The
Moving Survival
Guide

Help Us Keep This Guide Up to Date

Every effort has been made by the author and editors to make this guide as accurate and useful as possible. However, many changes can occur after a guide is published—new products and information become available, regulations change, techniques evolve, etc.

We would love to hear from you concerning your experiences with this guide and how you feel it could be improved and be kept up to date. While we may not be able to respond to all comments and suggestions, we'll take them to heart, and we'll make certain to share them with the author. Please send your comments and suggestions to the following address:

The Globe Pequot Press
Reader Response/Editorial Department
P.O. Box 480
Guilford, CT 06437

Or you may e-mail us at:

editorial@GlobePequot.com

Thanks for your input, and happy travels!

The Moving Survival Guide

All You Need to Know to Make Your Move Go Smoothly

Martha Poage

The Globe Pequot Press

GUILFORD, CONNECTICUT

To buy books in quantity for corporate use or incentives, call **(800) 962–0973, ext. 4551,** or e-mail **premiums@GlobePequot.com**

Text design by Mary Ballachino

Library of Congress Cataloging-in-Publication Data
Poage, Martha
    The moving survival guide / Martha Poage.—1st ed.
        p. cm
    ISBN 0-7627-3574-0
    1. Moving, Household. I. Title.

TX307.P63 2004
648'.9—dc22   2004051136

Manufactured in the United States of America
First Edition/First Printing

*This book is dedicated to my son, Brian, and my daughter, Meghan,
for all of their patience, love, and understanding during
the moving process and publication of this guide.*

Contents

Chapter Seven: Packing Days / 67

Chapter Eight: The Final Week / 85

Chapter Nine: Moving Day / 95

Chapter Ten: Delivery Day . . . and Unpacking / 103

Acknowledgments

After several moves, I realized that much of my adult life would undoubtedly be about moving if my husband was to continue his career as a corporate executive. I immediately decided to do something productive, to make moving worthwhile instead of complaining about my precarious life. The first thing I did was to learn from my past moves and not repeat a mistake on subsequent moves. Next I looked for a way to make this lifestyle a fun and rewarding experience for the entire family; otherwise we could not survive each move.

And finally, I decided to assist other people who want to move. Thus this book was born.

I especially want to thank my husband, Rob, and my children, Brian and Meghan, who inspired me to persist with my idea even as the challenges of moving intensified over the years. A fond thanks to my mother-in-law, Hazel Poage, for her friendship, writing advice, and encouragement along the way. A special thanks to Nancy Freeborn, a high school classmate, for presenting my book to Mary Norris, who gave me a chance to make my publishing goal a reality. And finally, thanks to my editor, Paula Brisco, who took my idea and brought it to life.

Introduction

Congratulations on your move!

This is a thrilling time in your life, a time of fond farewells and new beginnings. No matter how near or how far you are moving, careful and organized planning is the key to maintaining the excitement in your moving experience. Whether you are simply contemplating a move or are only a week away from moving day, this is the guide for you.

I have moved my family across the country seven times in ten years as a result of my husband's career. I completely understand and sympathize with the inconveniences moving imposes upon your family, your friends, your job, and your life, and I want to help you through this complex process. I use this guide myself to ensure that each of my family's moves is a success!

The United States is the most mobile society in the world. It is estimated that each year nearly 20 percent of the population relocates. Roughly speaking, forty million Americans moved in 2001. Approximately 800,000 of these moves can be contributed to job-related transfers. So don't feel that you are alone. Whether you are moving locally or across the country, relocation is no simple matter. The adventure of the new can quickly lead to panic and anxiety if you are not prepared. You will love to move if you use this step-by-step guide to plan your move.

Relocation Requires Planning

Relocating is a huge task for a single individual and an immense challenge when the entire family is involved. The individual needs of each family member must be considered. Even if your move is a corporate relocation, almost everything but the heavy lifting, packing, and unpacking will be your responsibility. It can be a stressful and emotional time for all involved, and planning ahead is the only way to stay in control of the situation.

The Moving Survival Guide was written to help you plan the many details of your move, help you make informed decisions, and keep you organized throughout these busy and emotional premoving months. The useful information will eliminate many unexpected situations that otherwise could arise, and thus your move will go more smoothly. This is not a book that you need to read from cover to cover. It is intended to be a hands-on workbook to make your life easier during your move.

The Moving Survival Guide is your road map to success. Keep it with you at all times, along with your sense of humor, and your move will be more successful. You'll find page after page of practical advice, inspirational tips, and answers to questions. There are month-to-month planning calendars, detailed checklists, and worksheets to help budget your time and money. This book also features the most comprehensive moving checklist ever published! And since job-related transfers are not always welcomed by all family members, I include detailed information to make corporate relocation less traumatic and more successful for the entire family.

Browse through this book chapter by chapter to get an understanding of the job that lies ahead of you. You will be surprised at how much more pleasant moving becomes when you are prepared every step of the way. Your move will definitely be more organized and less stressful if you follow this guide.

CHAPTER ONE

The Moving Mind-Set

Moving is a physical process—and a demanding one at that. Moving is also a state of mind. You can make the process go more smoothly if you develop the moving mind-set. What is this mind-set? It's a positive attitude, a recognition that challenges lie ahead but that you and your family can meet them. When you develop the moving mind-set, you take the opportunity to celebrate change with friends and family, to embrace your new community, and to help your children (and yourself) cope with the moving blues.

The moving mind-set is also your commitment to staying on track from the beginning of the moving process until you are completely settled into your new community. This book will lead you through this process and not leave you dangling on any issues that may arise along the way. Routinely reviewing the Comprehensive Moving Checklist located in Appendix A is part of this process. The checklist is included as a quick reference so that no detail of your move will be overlooked.

Maintaining the moving mind-set is often a challenge, especially for those of us who follow a partner's career moves. I am the "trailing spouse" as defined in the book *Love and Money* by Jeff D. Opdyke. I have followed my husband on his career up the corporate ladder and abandoned my own career to move around the country and raise our family. I have made friends only to lose most of them each time I moved, decorated houses only to sell them the following year, learned my way around town only to erase that mental road map and relearn it in yet another town. When my children lost their friends and social standing in school, I lost my identity. I have been elated over some moves and cried over others. I have been lonely and isolated many times. I have started from square one seven times. When I walk into a school meeting, no one knows who I am. When I watch a soccer game, I sit alone. It hurts when our children are always the new kids who don't get invited to birthday parties and sleepovers. However, I am a survivor.

There is a positive side to being the trailing spouse, in spite of all the drawbacks. Being the observer, I've learned a great deal about people and how communities in America change from place to place. I've met many fascinating and knowledgeable people. Our children have become more social and outgoing. They have a better understanding of what is important in life. I have lived in some of the most beautiful places in America. My husband's career provides us with an affluent lifestyle and enables us to give our children a great education. Our family has learned to stay connected to each other, and we bond more tightly together with each move. Since I no longer bring home a paycheck, I made it my goal to make money in the real estate market each time we move. Writing this moving guide has also given my life purpose and provided a way to help other people in my situation. If you are a trailing spouse, you are part of an American phenomenon; you must move from being a star in your own life to a supporting player in your spouse's life. The successful players learn how to become a star in each new situation, in spite of the fact that they no longer call the shots. This book will help you achieve that goal.

Celebrate with Style

Moving is a time of change, so why not celebrate the change with style? Here are some of my favorite tried-and-true ways to start a move off on a positive foot.

Plan a Going-Away Party or Two!

Celebrate this new milestone in your life with a party. Make a list of everyone you and your family members want to invite. Plan the party on a date when most people will be able to attend, and hold it well in advance of your moving date. Make sure children are included on the list, or plan a separate party for them and their friends. You may want to have a separate intimate dinner party or outdoor barbecue for really close friends.

Visit Favorite Places

To better prepare youngsters for an upcoming move, photograph them at their favorite places, such as the playground, their best friend's house, or McDonald's. Ask your children to say good-bye to these special spots and to their friends. After you

List of People to Invite to the Party

1. _____   11. _____

2. _____   12. _____

3. _____   13. _____

4. _____   14. _____

5. _____   15. _____

6. _____   16. _____

7. _____   17. _____

8. _____   18. _____

9. _____   19. _____

10. _____   20. _____

move, show your children the photos to remind them of all the fun they had at these places. Then say, "Let's find a fun new place." Capture their imagination by leading them on a new adventure. Take photos at these places and of them playing with their new friends. Show your children the new pictures and explain that they can have fun and friends in *both* places. This will help kids adjust to the move more quickly.

Each person in the family can help complete the following list. Places to list on the chart can include playground, zoo, library, favorite restaurant, children's museum, school, park, friend's house, shopping mall, or swimming pool.

Say Good-Bye

Even if you've had a going-away party, don't forget to say good-bye to your favorite neighbors. Give them your new address and phone number so you can all stay in touch. And make sure your children give their friends your new street and e-mail

List of Places to Visit before I Move

1. _____   6. _____

2. _____   7. _____

3. _____   8. _____

4. _____   9. _____

5. _____   10. _____

address—children get really excited when they receive mail at their new home. Encourage correspondence. A pen pal is a good learning experience, one that will help children with their writing and communication skills. Writing also provides a bridge from their old life to their new life and fills the gap until they are able to make new friends. And it's a quiet activity for them to do when you are busy unpacking.

My husband and I moved every year when our children were in preschool through third grade. To make the transition to the new place more enjoyable, I would make each child a cake to take to school on his or her last day. The cake was decorated with an outline of the new state and its name. It would also say "Good-bye Meghan" or "Good-bye Brian" and include a picture of something about the new state. When we moved to California, for instance, one cake was decorated with a yellow sun and the other with a surfboard. It was a great way for my kids to celebrate the upcoming move and say good-bye to their friends at school.

Time Management Is Key

You can take control over your move through good time management. The following month-to-month planning calendar shows you how to record all aspects of your move. The examples here illustrate how I scheduled one of my family's moves. (You'll find blank calendars in Appendix B.) Fill in the appropriate month and dates to customize your calendar. Since dates may change as you are planning your move, it is best to use a pencil when filling out your calendar.

At a minimum, fill in the following key dates on your planning calendar:

- Notify landlord in writing of move-out date (renters).
- Obtain loan preapproval.
- Sign the real estate contract to sell the current house.
- Accept or decline the company buyout offer.
- Sign the real estate contract to purchase a new house.
- Sign the rental contract on a new apartment and pay applicable fees (renters).
- Obtain a moving estimate.
- Obtain loan final approval.
- Schedule the house appraisal.
- Schedule house closing date(s), location(s), and time(s).
- Obtain new auto and homeowner's insurance coverage.
- Make travel arrangements (if moving long distance).
- Schedule packing days.
- Schedule moving day.
- Schedule final walk-through of the new house.
- Schedule move in and unpacking.
- Submit change of address form to the local post office or complete it online.
- Call to verify that your loan has been funded by the required date.
- Cancel utilities at the old location and add utilities to the new location.
- Cancel home deliveries and services.
- Obtain new driver's license and motor vehicle license (if moving out of state).
- Submit claim form to the moving company for any missing or damaged property.
- Obtain security deposit refund after you have moved out of your apartment (renters).

Planning Calendar

Month: _____July_____ Months to go: _____2_____

Sunday	Monday	Tuesday	Wednesday	Thursday	Friday	Saturday
___	___	1 House ready to put on the market	2	3 Meet with agent to sign real estate contracts	4 Holiday	5 House goes into the MLS listing today
6 Review moving checklist	7 House showings today 10:00 A.M. 3:00 P.M.	8 House showing today 11:00 A.M.	9 Receive offer on house	10 Call relocation counselor about offer	11 Accept offer on house	12
13	14 Search for a mortgage loan	15 Schedule house-hunting trip	16 House inspection today	17 Obtain moving estimate	18 Choose a mortgage lender	19
20	21 Request mortgage prequalification letter	22 Fill out new house wish list	23	24 Receive mortgage prequalification letter	25 Moving agent to examine household inventory	26
27 Leave for house-hunting trip	28 Check out new school district	29 New house search	30 New house search	31 New house search	___	___

Planning Calendar

Month: _____August_____ Months to go: _____1_____

Sunday	Monday	Tuesday	Wednesday	Thursday	Friday	Saturday
—	—	—	—	—	1 Put offer down on new house	2 Return from house-hunting trip
3 Negotiate new house offer	4 New house offer accepted	5 Schedule new house inspection	6 Obtain new home-owner's insurance	7 Submit final mortgage loan docu-ments	8 Schedule cancellation of home services/ deliveries	9 Make airline reservations
10	11 Schedule packing and moving dates	12 Schedule new house appraisal	13 Schedule extra vehicle for shipment	14	15 Arrange for the transfer of pets	16 Review moving checklist
17	18 Receive final approval on loan	19 Take school transfer forms to school	20	21 Complete house inspection items	22 Packers arrive	23 Make hotel arrangements
24 Review the Final Week Checklist	25 Packers Cancel and add utilities	26 Packers Submit change of address form to the post office	27 Load the moving van Review moving day tips	28 Load the moving van Finish cleaning the house	29 Begin cross-country drive to new state	30

Planning Calendar

Month: _____September_____ Months to go: _____0_____

Sunday	Monday	Tuesday	Wednesday	Thursday	Friday	Saturday
	1 Holiday	2 Call relocation counselor about closing process	3 Arrive at new state Call to verify that loan has funded	4 Final walk-through New house cleaning	5 Delivery Day—move in	6 Delivery Day—partial unpack
7 Explore the new neighbor-hood	8 Unpackers The kids start at their new school	9 Unpackers	10 Take a drive to learn your way around town	11 Review moving checklist	12	13 Celebrate the 1st Saturday night in new home
14	15 Obtain new auto insurance	16	17 Mail moving receipts to the relocation company for reimbursement	18	19	20 Find a new health club
21	22	23	24 Locate new doctors and dentists	25	26 Obtain a new driver's license	27
28 Review moving checklist for uncompleted items	29	30 Register motor vehicles	1 Arrange for the transfer of medical records	2	3 Make list of items damaged or missing	4

Live Out Your Fantasies!

How else can you maintain the moving mind-set? Choose a different style house each time you move. If you have the time, build your dream house. Or better yet, pretend that you are on a paid vacation for a year or two and use your time accordingly: Explore all of the local sites and tourist attractions in your community. Dine at local restaurants, attend local fairs, and experience the unique culture that each area has to offer. Make friends with the local residents, visit national landmarks and museums in the area, and discover vacation destinations. Visit new stores and buy unusual furniture and accessories to give your house that eclectic, well-traveled look. Buy furniture and decorator items to suit your taste, not just your current home's floor plan, since the architectural style of your house may change the next time you move.

Make It Home Sweet Home

Moving is a huge job. You will be exhausted, both physically and emotionally. It may take six months to a year before you feel at home in your new location. If you experience these feelings don't blame yourself for your uneasiness. It's just a phase that you may have to go through before you reestablish your sense of security. Setting up a new routine and making new friends can bring comfort and stability back into your life during this transitional period. Spending time together as a family exploring your new environment can be fun, educational, and therapeutic. Staying in contact with loved ones can also ease the transition. Writing letters or sending e-mail to friends in your old neighborhood will help to put your feelings about the move into perspective. If you send a message to your friends, you will almost certainly get notes back in return, and that will help you feel connected to your old life. Before you know it, your new place will feel like Home Sweet Home.

Shed No More Tears!

As soon as I find out that I am moving, I use this moving guide as a way to stay focused on the job that lies ahead. It is not until the new house is unpacked, my husband heads off to work, and my children leave for school every morning that it finally sinks in that I have lost my old life and the daily contact with my friends. This is when I try to focus on getting our house back in order, locating new things for my family to do, and starting my own new routine to make my life feel comfortable and normal again. The feeling of loneliness always hits at some point in a move, but remember that you are the one in control of how long it will last.

Get Involved

Getting involved in your new community is the quickest way to feeling settled. Learn to appreciate that change can make your life richer and more exciting. Locate a community newsletter or local newspaper, look in the front pages of your local telephone directory, or call the chamber of commerce or newcomers' group for information about your new community. You might call Welcome Wagon at (800) 77–WELCOME (935–2663), or log on to www.homestore.com for a free Welcome Wagon gift. If you are a new mother, join a community play group. Volunteer at your local church, school, or hospital. Visit the local library, community college, or university to find out about adult education classes. Exercising during this hectic time will also help reduce your stress level. Join a club or a gym. Go jogging, bike riding, or in-line skating around your new neighborhood. Head out for a stroll and introduce yourself to your new neighbors. Take your dog for a walk and go exploring. Invite family, friends, and people from work to see your new home. If you enjoy being social and like to cook and entertain, start or join a cooking club, wine-tasting club, or progressive dinner party group. Help plan a block party in your new neighborhood, or join a bridge club or bunco group. The sooner you get into a new routine, the sooner you will feel settled.

Find the Unlikely Friend

New friends can be found in unlikely situations. I once met a woman at the community pool, and she became my friend for years, even after my family moved away. We have daughters one year apart in age, and we shared laughter and stories about our moving experiences. She too was new to the neighborhood. New friends do not replace old friends, but unlikely friends fulfill our needs at different points in our lives, and they may even develop into friendships that last a lifetime.

When you are the newcomer to the neighborhood, don't expect the neighbors to invite you over first. People are busy today, juggling demanding jobs and children's complex schedules. If you want to make friends more quickly, you must take the initiative to introduce yourself and to invite people over to your house first. This applies to children too! Children are more likely to make friends quickly if you walk over to the neighbor's house, knock on the door, and introduce yourself to other parents in the neighborhood.

Lost Again?

If you have moved to a completely new area, you will get lost frequently while you try to learn your way around town. This may be very frustrating and stressful. When you are new to an area, keep a map with you at all times, or download directions from the Internet before you set out to find to a new destination. Review the map before you leave the house; this will help you get to new places more quickly and painlessly. Call ahead of time and ask for clear driving directions to avoid getting lost. Stop and ask for directions if you do get disoriented. Or take a completely different approach and spend time driving around without a destination in mind just to get a feel for the region. Eventually you will acquire a mental map of the area, and your frustration level will drop each time you reach your destination successfully. When you finally know your way, you will feel more comfortable in your new surroundings.

Moving over the Summer

If you have moved over the summer, as many people do, unpack the necessities only and then enjoy the rest of the summer. This is especially appropriate if you have children home on summer vacation. You don't need to spoil a child's summer holi-

Martha's Moving Survival Tips

Beware of Mother Nature. As we all know, Mother Nature is unpredictable. When I was moving from Colorado to Washington in February, the Snoqualmie Pass was closed for three days due to a huge snowstorm. The moving company informed me that the van would be three days late! There is nothing you can do in this situation but just sit back and relax. Spend the extra time sightseeing in your new town, playing with your children, getting to know the new neighborhood, cleaning your new house, watching a movie, or reading a good book. Consider this unexpected break a time to give your body a chance to recover before the second wave of moving hits you . . . the unpacking!

days by spending every day unpacking boxes. Children need extra love and attention more than ever after being uprooted from friends and familiar surroundings. If you are not a working parent, there will be plenty of time to decorate and perfect your house in the fall when the children return to school. If you are a working parent, consider hiring someone to help you get settled more quickly. Then use your free time to take the children exploring in your new neighborhood and community. Enjoy this special time together as a family before the children have homework, extracurricular activities, and new friends knocking at the door.

Overcoming the Moving Blues

It is only human nature to miss the things that you liked about your old home, friends, and life. And you will probably even miss the things that you disliked about your old life! For example: After you move you will not remember that your next-door neighbor's dog was annoying. You will only remember that you miss having a familiar neighbor. It takes time to feel comfortable in a new home and community. Even after you have chosen what seemed to be the perfect location, you will probably find fault with it once you move in. When things go wrong in your life, you may even believe you made a mistake in your relocation decision. However, don't be so hard on yourself! Keep a positive attitude, and as each day passes you will gradually overcome obstacles. If you did your homework before the move, trust your instincts and be confident that you made the best decision possible.

Understand Your Children's Needs

Young children are resilient and will usually get excited about moving if their parents act like they are excited about the move. So set the right example! Start by reading children a few positive books on the subject, such as *The Berenstain Bears Moving Day*, by Stan and Jan Berenstain, and *Oh, The Places You'll Go!*, by Dr. Seuss. You can help by giving children a sense of control over their new environment. When possible, let them choose their new bedrooms, and set those rooms up promptly. Young children will adjust to their new surroundings more quickly if their bedroom is put back together as soon as possible, their toys are unpacked, and they know where to find their favorite snacks in the kitchen. They will feel a sense of security knowing that some things in their life have not changed. On the other hand, teenage children may use this opportunity to request that their rooms be completely redecorated. Hooking up the television, DVD player, Xbox, and Internet will get teenagers settled in quickly.

To get children excited about the move, take a tour of the new house, neighborhood, and school. Let them take pictures during the tour so that they can gradually get adjusted to their new surroundings. The more familiar they become with the new community, the less apprehensive and more cooperative they will be during the move. Encourage older children to track down information about the new community on the Internet and to keep in touch with their old friends via e-mail and instant messaging. Help your children to make friends. Encourage them to invite new friends over to your house so you can get to know them and meet their parents. You may find that you have something in common with their parents, which may lead to a new friendship for yourself.

Changing schools can sometimes be traumatic for children, especially during the teenage years. If you have control over when to move, it is a good idea to weigh the social problems caused by a summer move against the uncertain academic drawbacks of relocating during the school year. The most difficult issue for teenagers is having to give up all of their friends and planned activities. To teenagers, their life stops dead at the very mention of a move, and they perceive no light at the end of the tunnel if their current social life is going to end. They become confused about how to tell their friends that they are moving because they themselves are so confused about the idea of relocation and they do not want to lose the friendships that mean the world to them. This is when a few books may help, especially if this is a first move. Appropriate reading on this subject for teenagers includes *Who Moved My Cheese? For Teens,* by Spencer Johnson; *Chicken Soup for the Teenage Soul on Tough Stuff,* by Jack Canfield, Mark Victor Hansen, and Kimberly Kirberger; and for girls, *The Girl's Life Guide to Growing Up,* edited by Karen Bokram and Alexis Sinex of *Girl's Life* magazine. These books may help teenagers realize that moving can be positive, an opportunity to do things in life that they never dreamed possible.

If your children are having trouble adjusting to their new school, call the guidance counselor and ask for advice on how to make the situation better. Encourage your children to talk to you about their grievances. Listen to your children's complaints, and try to help them through this difficult time. As each week passes, the situation should show improvement. If it doesn't, don't give up. Talk to other parents to see if other kids are having the same difficulties (it may only be an age-related problem, such as hormones). If all else fails, seek counseling elsewhere, or look for alternative schools that may suit your child's needs better.

Seek Professional Help If Necessary

If someone from your family or you are suffering from adjustment disorder, consult an expert for help if the following symptoms persist: bed wetting (in children), depression, mood swings, nightmares, personality changes, and sleeplessness. Talk to your spouse, employer, or doctor about the situation and seek counseling. It is estimated that 37 percent of job-related moves fail because the family does not form new relationships or set down permanent roots in the new location, or because of other family-related circumstances. In many of these cases, the employees quit their jobs, and many of these families return to their previous location. Moving again may be the right thing to do in difficult situations.

Martha's Moving Survival Tips

Creative ways to notify long-distance friends of your move. If you move as frequently as I do, you will eventually have friends all over the country. Each time you move, these friends will want to know all the details. There are many commercial cards readily available that you can purchase to announce your move. But if you are creative, like my daughter, you can design your own moving announcement on the computer and even send it via e-mail. Alternatively, I have used our family's yearly Christmas newsletter to inform friends of our latest move. I even include a humorous poem, such as "The Twelve Days of Christmas, Arizona Style," to make the letter more amusing. Sometimes I make up the wording; other times someone else has written the words for that state and I use that. Any of these techniques are practical ways to notify your friends of your move and to be entertaining at the same time.

CHAPTER TWO

Three Months to Go: Let's Get Organized

In the ideal world, you would start preparing for a move three months in advance. But if you are working on a tighter schedule (as often happens), you can still follow one of the most crucial steps: getting organized. That's what this chapter is all about.

I know firsthand how important organization can be to a move. When I was married, I had my files and my husband had his files. Then we started adding to those files as each tax season passed, as we built our first house (boxes and boxes of papers were accumulated during this process), and when our two children were born. Before we knew it, we had a mess on our hands. After my family's first move, I realized that I didn't even know what was in most of those boxes anymore. That was when I knew it was time to get organized.

One of the hardest parts about getting organized is deciding where to begin. Since paperwork seems to be the first thing that overtakes our desks and countertops, let's start by making files to contain the clutter. Then we can move on to tossing out papers that we no longer need and organizing the rest of our household items.

Getting organized either comes naturally, or it can be an agonizing experience. Either way, this chapter will help you to get organized more quickly and efficiently.

Create a Manageable Filing System

File information in file folders, a three-ring binder, or a file box. All three systems work effectively. Include file categories such as:

Automobile registration	Landscape maintenance
Bank statements	Medical records
Business cards	Miscellaneous
Church registration	Mortgage or rent payments
Club memberships	Moving documents
Credit card statements	Paychecks
Dental records	Professional organizations
Frequent-flier accounts	Property taxes
Homeowners' association	School report cards
Household receipts	Taxes (state and federal)
Insurance	Travel documents/receipts
Investment statements	Utilities

File business cards in a three-ring binder in plastic sheets designed for business cards.

Separate your utility records into categories: electric/gas, water/ garbage, telephone/wireless phone, newspaper, security system, cable TV, Internet service provider, etc.

File moving documents by category: escrow company or law firm, inspection company, moving/relocation company, mortgage company, real estate agency.

Martha's Moving Survival Tips

Boxes, boxes, and more boxes. The first time my family moved across the country, we packed everything ourselves to save money. I began packing three months ahead of time, but since I was working full-time and raising two babies, I wasn't able to pack until the children were asleep at night. To complicate matters, my husband had already relocated and could only help me pack every three weeks when he returned home. To say the least, on moving day I was unprepared and in a panic. When the moving van pulled away, there was hardly room in my car for my two children—it was nearly filled with miscellaneous items that hadn't been packed or loaded onto the van. That was a nightmare I'll never repeat! I've learned to be prepared.

What to Toss, What to Keep for Tax Reasons

The following are recommendations for saving financial and legal documents. Since tax rules change from year to year, always check with your accountant or go to www.irs.ustreas.gov for additional information.

Tax Documents

To stay organized all year long, collect all tax documents received throughout the year and place them in a large envelope in your home office. Label the envelope "Tax Documents Year ____." Keep your tax records in a filing cabinet or portable file box. In most cases, the Internal Revenue Service (IRS) has three years from the date on which your income tax return was due to request an audit. (If you underreported your income by more then 25 percent, the IRS has six years. If the agency suspects fraud or if you didn't file at all, there is no auditing deadline.)

Investment Records

You must be able to document when you bought an asset and how much you paid for it, and when you sold it and how much you sold it for.

Credit Cards and Statements

Credit card accounts need to be canceled if you no longer use particular credit cards It is not enough to cut up and throw away an expired card. You must call the credit card company and request cancellation of your account to prevent the possibility of unauthorized charges to your account. It is your job to protect your own credit status.

The only rule for retaining credit card statements is that you keep any statement that shows a purchase for a tax-deductible item.

Relocation Expense Receipts

Unreimbursed expenses of moving your personal effects and household goods and traveling to a new job location may be tax deductible if the distance and time tests are met. Job-hunting costs and commuting costs to a temporary workplace may also be deductible. (Consult your tax guide or tax accountant for the most recent tax laws on this subject.) Relocation expenses may include:

- Airline tickets and rental car and hotel receipts
- Moving personal effects and household goods and automobile-expense receipts
- Mileage records, parking fees, and toll receipts

Settlement Statement

In your escrow paperwork you will find your final settlement statement, also referred to as the U.S. Department of Housing and Urban Development (HUD) Report. This document will provide information needed to complete your income tax return. Deductible expenses may include prepaid mortgage interest and property taxes when buying or selling a home, and mortgage points or a loan origination fee if it is prepaid interest solely for the use of the loan money, not services.

Receipts for Automobile Licensing Fees

Automobile licensing and registration fees may contain tax-deductible expenses in some states. (Consult your tax guide or tax accountant for the most recent tax laws that apply to your state.)

Receipts for Charitable Donations

Clothing, household goods, and automobiles donated to a charity, and books donated to a library are tax-deductible items. Use prices at thrift or consignment stores to determine value (or use 20 percent of the original costs). It is best to keep receipts for all donations; however, you are legally required by the IRS to have a written receipt for donations valued over $250.

Timetable for Storing Financial and Legal Documents

How long should you keep documents? Here's a summary:

Property records: purchase/sales contract, deeds, titles, and home-improvement receipts. Keep for four years after the sale or due date of the tax return affected by the sale.

Investment records: stocks, options, bonds, and mutual funds. Keep for four years after the sale or due date of the tax return.

Tax return backup documents: original receipts and statements and other supporting documents. Keep for four years after filing or due date of the tax return.

Tax returns: Keep until anything ever related to the tax return has been disposed of, plus four years from the date of filing. (Copies of previously filed tax returns can be retrieved from the IRS if you have the address at which you lived in the year the tax return was filed. In some instances, it may take several months to obtain this copy.)

Retirement plan and insurance records: IRAs, Keogh plans, pension plans, other retirement plans, insurance policies, and such other contracts. Keep documents until all transactions have been fully completed and/or all funds have been withdrawn, plus three years (which sometimes means indefinitely). This would apply to records of all contributions, distributions, rollovers, and tax-free exchanges.

Bank records: statements and canceled checks. Canceled checks and statements, except for those checks and statements documenting tax-deductible expenses, can be thrown out as soon as you verify that your statements are correct. Tax-related records should be filed with your tax return documents.

Legal documents: birth certificates or adoption records, military records, marriage and divorce records, custody agreements, and proof of naturalization. Keep these permanently.

Protect Important Documents

Include the following types of documents in a portable fireproof safe or store in a safe-deposit box. Refer to the Comprehensive Moving Checklist in Appendix A for legal, insurance, and medical issues regarding your move.

- Last will and testament and living trust
- Insurance policies: auto, recreational vehicles, life, homeowner's, and renter's
- Stock certificates, stock option agreements, and savings bonds
- Medical records
- Certificates: birth, marriage, death, and religious
- Passports
- Motor vehicle certificates of title
- Appraisal documents
- Computer inventory diskette
- Computer financial records diskette
- Undeveloped film or CD of household inventory
- Irreplaceable photo negatives
- Social Security cards and documents
- Title policy and property deed

Organizing Step-by-Step

If you organize your belongings before you move, you will have an easier time find-ing items at the new location. You will be able to locate critical objects when you need them instead of going into a mad panic looking for them. More importantly, the moving company will be able to provide a more accurate estimate for the cost of your move if you are organized, and that may result in substantial savings to you.

- Put photos in chronological order in photo boxes or in acid-free photo albums. (Store away from light, heat, and humidity.)

- Place home videos, DVDs, and music CDs in video boxes or on a shelf.

- Store computer software CD-ROMs and diskettes in a box or on a rack.

- Place miscellaneous nails, screws, tacks, picture hooks, etc., in your toolbox or in a plastic container with small compartments.

- Store children's daily school papers in a large plastic box. (Preserve children's artwork in an acid-free box or briefcase. Label and store it in a dark closet.)

- Organize your memorabilia collection so that it is displayed properly.

- Sort recipes. Type miscellaneous handwritten recipes on the computer and then print and file them in a three-ring notebook. Then file the recipes you cut out of magazines in this notebook. Buy plastic page covers and insert each page into your notebook to keep recipes clean and orderly. If you want to be even more organized, type a table of contents page and place it at the beginning of your notebook so you can locate recipes more quickly.

- Streamline your closets. Closet specialists say the goal is to make space visible, accessible, and manageable. Think of the saying, "Out of sight, out of mind." It applies to your closets and drawers too! If you can't find something, you won't use it.

- Dispose of clothing that no longer fits and put seasonal clothing in plastic garment bags, boxes, or a cedar cabinet in the garage, base-ment, or attic.

- Organize your shoes and shoeboxes. Label your shoeboxes or take your shoes out of their original cardboard boxes and place them in clear acrylic shoeboxes.

- Store toys in large, clear plastic storage containers, in a toy box, or in a closet.

- Arrange your gift-wrap supplies and seasonal decorations in plastic storage containers, then place the containers on a shelf or store them in a closet.

- Organize your books and magazines. (Recycle old magazines and unwanted books.)

- Collect household appliance manuals and warranty information and store in one kitchen drawer, or put them in a three-ring binder, or place them in a filing cabinet or box.

- Sort your closets, drawers, and pantry so that items can be easily located.

- Purge and clean your medicine cabinet. Throw away all expired medications.

- Thoroughly clean your refrigerator and freezer at least every six months. Dispose of food that is moldy, past its expiration date, or that no one will ever eat. Keep your refrigerator clean and smelling fresh. Food will look more appetizing if the refrigerator is not cluttered.

- Organize your garage, basement, and attic. Discard items that you do not need.

Helpful Hints to Keep Your House Organized

I now organize my house step-by-step daily to make my life more efficient so that I don't have an overwhelming job preparing for the next move. When my house is for sale, I make sure that my family pays special attention to the items on this list so that my house will show at its best.

Staying organized especially helps during the school year when the kids bring home an endless amount of paperwork for me to review. A well maintained home is also a more enjoyable place for my family to live in and will make a better impression on the new guests that we will be inviting to our new house.

1. Hang up garments instead of leaving them on the floor, bed, or chair.

2. Hang up towels to dry.

3. Pick up dropped items.

4. Wipe up spills and messes when they occur.

5. Clean out the kitchen sink and wipe off the kitchen countertops as required.

6. Run the dishwasher when full.

7. Empty the dishwasher when clean.

8. Empty wastebaskets when full.

9. Wash accumulated dirty laundry. (Clean the lint screen in the dryer often.)

10. Fold clothes as soon as dryer cycle is complete so garments do not get wrinkled.

11. Iron clothes frequently so unmanageable piles do not accumulate.

12. Open, read, and discard or file the mail accordingly.

13. Place retired newspapers and magazines in the recycle bin.

14. File office paperwork weekly. Don't let unmanageable piles accumulate.

15. Clean the house at least every two weeks (vacuum, dust, clean the bathrooms and wash the floors), or hire someone else to do it.

16. Wash the sheets and towels every week or two, or as necessary.

17. Place books back on the bookshelf after reading them.

18. Return items to their rightful place when finished using them.

19. Discard broken or nonuseful items.

20. Throw away nonedible leftovers.

21. Return library books by their due date.

22. Return DVDs, video rentals, and video games on time.

23. Recycle extra metal hangers by returning them to the cleaners.

24. Put keys in the same place every time you put them down.

25. Hang up your coat when you take it off.

26. Push in your chair when leaving the table.

27. After purchasing new clothes, donate outgrown or out-of-style clothing to your favorite charity or to family and friends.

28. Hold a garage sale or donate items to a charitable organization at least once a year.

29. Replace burnt-out lightbulbs as required.

30. Spot clean soil spots on carpets immediately to prevent permanent stains.

31. Clean up after your pets often.

32. Remove seasonal decorations in a timely manner after the season ends.

33. Avoid purchasing unnecessary items just because they are on sale.

34. Assign chores to every member of the family to get the job done faster.

35. Buy some flowers to reward yourself for all of your hard work. Then relax and enjoy your lovely home!

Take Inventory

The first time my husband and I moved we had to put most of our belongings in storage until our new house was completed. When we finally received the rest of our furniture and boxes six months later, two or three of the boxes were missing. I had a hard time remembering what was in those boxes since I packed them myself and did not keep a record of what I packed. This was before I had completed an inventory list of our household items. When it came time to complete the claim form documenting what was missing, I was at a loss. It took me a few months and a lot of aggravation to determine what was in those missing boxes before I could submit my claim for reimbursement.

An inventory list is a useful tool in this type of situation or in the event of a household emergency such as theft or fire. If high-value inventory items are lost, appraisal documents for these items must be provided to the moving company or reimbursement will be denied. This lesson taught me to be prepared for the worst-case scenario when moving.

How do you prepare an inventory list? Once you've organized your paperwork and household, record the contents of your house, room by room. (Quicken Deluxe 2000 has a home inventory software program to track your possessions by room location. Save the information on a diskette and keep it in a fireproof safe.) Assign an appropriate value for each item and you will have a permanent record of the value of your personal assets. Take photographs or videotape your belongings to use as documentation for insurance purposes. Keep sales receipts for expensive purchases for insurance purposes also.

Your inventory should include these categories of household items:

- Furniture: indoor and outdoor
- Lamps

- Area rugs
- Window coverings
- Home electronics: stereo equipment, TV, VCR, DVD/video game player, and clocks
- Computer hardware: monitor, CPU, keyboard, printer, super disk, etc.
- Entertainment supplies: CDs, DVDs, tapes, home videos, video games, and camera
- Computer software: programs and games
- Clothing and shoes
- Linens: towels, sheets, comforters, blankets, tablecloths, cloth napkins, etc.
- Appliances: large and small
- China and dishes
- Pots and pans
- Kitchen utensils, silver, and flatware
- Glassware and crystal stemware
- Collectibles: antiques, artwork, sculptures, wine, coins, etc.
- Specialty items: piano, musical instruments, pool table, Ping-Pong table, grandfather clock, aquarium, telephone and answering machine, etc.
- Books and encyclopedias
- Memorabilia: photo albums, stamps, souvenirs, etc.
- Professional items: photographic equipment, telescope, binoculars, and video camera
- Furs, jewelry, and accessories
- Toys and play equipment
- Sports and recreational equipment: bicycles, golf clubs, tennis rackets, skis, etc.
- Hand and power tools
- Lawn, garden, and camping equipment: mower, snowblower, barbecue grill, tent, etc.
- Automobiles, boats, Jet Skis, motorcycles, recreational vehicles, etc.

CHAPTER THREE

Be a Motivated Seller

I have been told that I am every Realtor's dream. What are people talking about when they say this? It means that when I interview a Realtor or real estate agent to sell my house, I have already done my homework and have my house ready to put on the market. When you are a motivated seller, you try to impress your agent (the same way you are trying to impress a buyer) to sell your house at the highest price. Pretend that the agent is your first potential buyer. Remember that first impressions are everything, not only to a potential buyer but also to a real estate agent. If you want the agent to sell your property quickly and get top dollar, show him or her that you are a serious seller by the immaculate appearance of your home. In addition, remember that you and your agent are a team. You must both work hard and support each other during this emotional process.

If you do not have a real estate agent, you can use the Internet to locate an agent in your neighborhood at www.realtor.com or www.homestore.com, ask a neighbor for a reference, or talk to your relocation representative.

Refer to the Comprehensive Moving Checklist in Appendix A for legal issues concerning your real estate transactions.

Make Your House Show like a Model Home

The goal is to make your house show like a model home. There should be a place for everything and everything in its place. Builders know that model homes sell their houses. Not only are models clean and neat and orderly, but there is usually classical music playing in the background, the windows are spotless and sunlight is flooding into the house, and all of the light fixtures and lamps in the house are switched on. Sometimes there are cookies baking in the kitchen, a fire in the fireplace, or hot cider on the stove. People fall in love with model homes because they are impeccably decorated and beautifully landscaped. People are enthralled by a model home. Personal belongings—such as shampoo in the shower, toothbrushes on the countertop, dishrags in the sink, or dirty boots in the laundry room—are not scattered throughout the house. When people walk though a model home, they say to themselves, "I could live here!" Potential buyers can fall in love with your house if you replicate that formula for success.

Model homes are fun to explore! Go visit a few model homes in your area. Bring your camera and take pictures of your favorite creative ideas to use in your home. If you have been thinking about adding a few pieces of new furniture or accessories to your home, now is a good time to go shopping. If you are on a budget, look for furniture sales. Sometimes floor sale items can be delivered within a few days. Also look for a model-home furniture sale where you can often buy high-quality, unique furniture and accessories at greatly reduced prices. New, stylish furniture and accessories make a room look more inviting and dramatic.

Create a House with Curb Appeal

Start your house makeover on the outside. You will be more successful at getting potential buyers to come inside and look at your house if your house has curb appeal. To create a well-maintained exterior that shows pride of ownership, follow these simple guidelines:

- Keep lawns and hedges neatly trimmed.
- Pull weeds and plant flowers in the garden or in pots.
- Wash the windows.
- Sweep or hose down the walkways and driveway.
- Oil squeaky gate hinges and latches.
- Repair broken fences or crumbling walls.
- Remove dead branches from trees and prune if necessary.
- Touch up exterior trim around windows and doors.

■ Replace burnt-out lightbulbs and clean light fixtures.

■ Keep the garage door shut. (This creates a better appearance and deters theft.)

■ Rake leaves in the fall and clear the walkways.

■ Remove construction debris from your yard. (If you live in a neighborhood that is under construction, trash and debris may blow into your yard on windy days.)

■ Remove snow and ice from walkways, driveways, and steps in winter.

■ Place the For Sale sign in full view of the street and place sales brochures in the box. (Fill up the brochure box when it is empty.)

Enhance Your Home with Designer Touches

Once you get a potential buyer through the front door, you only have ten seconds to make a lasting impression. The front entrance to your home sets the stage for your home. Try to create a sense of awe that draws a person into your home. Welcome people with a fresh, clean, uncluttered look. Add a decorative rug, stunning piece of artwork, or plant at the entrance to add color and excitement to the area. Place a vase of fresh flowers or an artificial flower arrangement in the living room or on the kitchen island.

Try incorporating the following seven decorating basics into your home to create excitement and add pizzazz to an ordinary floor plan. If this job seems too overwhelming, contact a design professional. (Refer to Chapter Four for more information on this topic.) Also, browse through new magazines and books on interior decorating to get a few up-to-date ideas.

1. **Color.** This is the easiest and least expensive way to add vibrancy to a dull room. Apply a contrasting color to accent an area (known as a color block); hang attractive wallpaper; add interesting paint finishes such as faux, rage, or sponge paint; or paint a border or a mural on the wall.

2. **Focal point.** Every room needs a focal point. An architectural feature, a piece of furniture, or a piece of artwork can create a resting spot for the eye.

3. **Furniture arrangement.** Group furniture into a functional arrangement to make rooms appear larger.

4. **Lighting.** Use natural sunlight, lamps, spotlights, and overhead lighting to accent a room. Turn on all lights during a house showing.

5. **Pattern.** Tastefully coordinate different patterns to create intrigue.

6. **Scale.** The trick is to make a room appear larger by adding larger pieces of furniture and accessories, especially in rooms with small spaces.

7. **Texture.** Make a room appear more interesting by complementing smooth textures with rough textures through the use of different fabrics, furniture styles, accessories, floor coverings, paint, and wallpaper.

Staging a Home

In affluent areas of the country where the real estate market is booming and real estate is very expensive, many sellers "stage a home." This means that the owners remove all of their own furniture and belongings and move out. They then rent beautiful furniture and matching accessories (including bedding, pillows, area rugs, plants, and artwork) to make their house show its best. They try to make the house look like a model home. Many real estate agents and relocation specialists can provide this type of service for you.

When builders are trying to sell luxury homes in a slower market, they sometimes decorate them with new furniture and hold a 50 percent off model-home furniture sale to attract buyers. By attracting people who are looking for new furniture at a discounted price, they are also hoping to attract a buyer for the house. This may be a good place for you to purchase reasonably priced items for your home.

Repair, Replace, Renew

Once you've applied the broad brushstrokes, it's time to attend to the details.

- Repair drawer and cabinet doors that stick, squeak, or don't hang or open properly.
- Replace loose, broken, or cracked tiles.
- Replace burnt-out lightbulbs in the light fixtures and appliances.
- Replace windows that have broken vacuum seals or cracks.
- Repair leaky roof damage promptly to prevent internal drywall problems.
- Repair drywall stress cracks.

- Repair leaky faucets and toilets that run.

- Repair curtain rods that are not hanging properly.

- Repair window coverings that do not open and shut properly.

- Steam clean or replace worn-out carpet with a neutral-color, quality carpet.

- Clean the bathrooms and hang decorative, clean towels neatly on the towel bars.

- Clean the chandeliers and light fixtures.

- Dust, vacuum, and mop the floors.

- Remove dead bugs and debris from overhead ceiling lights.

- Dust high ledges and overhangs.

- Clean the top of the refrigerator and the inside if it will be sold with the house.

- Remove all items from the exterior of the refrigerator door.

- Clean appliances and make sure they are in proper working order.

- Remove cobwebs from ceilings, chandeliers, and windows.

- Put away all personal bathroom items in a cabinet or drawer.

- Declutter countertops and shelves.

- Arrange books, knickknacks, curios, dishes, and glassware neatly on shelves or cabinets.

- Make the sinks, faucets, knobs, mirrors, floors, and appliances shine.

Make Your Home Accessible to Potential Buyers

Now that the house is spotless, what's next? If you're a motivated seller, you want your house accessible to potential buyers to ensure a quick sale. Since a lockbox provides the easiest access to your home, grant your real estate agent permission to put one on your home. (Agents from cooperating companies are given your lockbox code only after verification of their broker identification number.) It is recommended that you leave the house during a showing and let the agent handle the situation. Potential buyers usually feel more comfortable and tend to spend more time looking at a home if the owner is not on the premises.

Carefully secure all valuable items during house showings, including paperwork for any other offers on the house. Place the Realtor's sales sheets in an obvious place. Put your pets in a cage, outside, or in the garage during house showings. Clean animal litter boxes so that they smell fresh. Pick up animal waste in the yard. Place a sign on the garage door such as: "Please do not let our dog/cat in the house." Avoid cooking meals that may cause an unpleasant, lingering odor.

Make your house available to show at all reasonable times, unless there are extenuating circumstances, i.e., someone is sick, there has been an accident in the house, etc. Many buyers are from out of town and have a tight schedule. If it is inconvenient to see your house, they may cross it off their list. Don't let this situation happen to you. Be a motivated seller!

Request an Agents' Preview

Ask your real estate agent to hold an "agents' preview." The more agents who preview your house, the more showings you should get, assuming that your house is presentable and priced competitively. In a good market, between ten and fifteen agents should preview your house at the preview. In today's market, agents are the marketing key to selling your house quickly: They have access to the multiple listing service, and they can locate the most qualified buyers for your home.

Review the Sales Sheet

Upon your approval, the real estate agent will usually place a For Sale sign in your front yard. (*Note:* Some estates and neighborhoods do not permit signs.) This sign often includes a box to hold sales sheets.

Every real estate office has its own style of sales sheet. The sheet is intended to provide a brief description of your house. It usually has a colored photograph of the exterior of your home and sometimes includes interior photographs of certain areas. Sales sheets become more elaborate as the price of the house increases. For privacy reasons, the price of the house is not always included on the sales sheet. A potential buyer can call the agent listed on the sales sheet to request the sale price of a home.

Attachments to the sheet may include the floor plan, the house size (number of rooms or square footage), and the lot size (square footage or number of acres); a page documenting the accomplishments of the home's builder and/or architect (if

Martha's Moving Survival Tips

Understand your agent's terms. The term *winterize* has multiple meanings to real estate agents. Three winterizing procedures are performed to drain the pipes to prevent freezing and bursting of such pipes when the temperature drops below freezing in the winter.

Winterize can mean winterize your sprinkler system: "Turn off and drain the sprinkler system pipes for the winter." It can mean winterize your pool or hot tub: "Turn off and drain the pipes to the swimming pool or hot tub for the winter." Or it can mean winterize your house: "Turn off the water, drain, and fill the pipes with antifreeze in the house for the winter." It can also mean that your vacation home is heated in the cold winter months.

Don't let your entire house get winterized when you only want your sprinkler system and pool winterized. Know the terms!

they have an outstanding reputation in the area), and a sheet with a local area map indicating the location and names of the school districts. The latter page can be extremely helpful to out-of-town buyers with school-age children.

If your home is located in an area with a homeowners' association, a list of the amenities and monthly dues may also be included on the sales sheet. The list of amenities may read like this: "Gated, tree-lined community with sidewalks, two separate swimming pool areas, sports fields, basketball court, bicycle and running trails, children's playground equipment, picnic tables, gazebo, and maintenance all for only $139/month."

Your agent may ask you to review the sales sheet and photograph of your house before printing to ensure that you are satisfied with the sheet's appearance and content. If any information listed on the sales sheet is incorrect, promptly inform your agent so that a correction can be made before the sheet is printed. Under the remarks section, you may want to embellish the agent's sales sheet if you feel that additional details would be helpful to a potential buyer. But remember, space is limited on the sales sheet, so keep additional comments brief and to the point.

To avoid any misunderstandings or legal disputes, it's extremely important to list exclusions—that is, items that *will not* remain with the residence. Examples of possible exclusions include: chandeliers, draperies, curtains and rods, refrigerator, washer and dryer, freestanding garage storage cabinets, outdoor play equipment, and outdoor decorative pots and statues.

Once you've approved the sales sheet and your agent has begun using it, check the sales sheet box frequently to make sure there are plenty of sheets inside. Call your agent promptly if the box needs to be refilled.

Information Included in a Sales Sheet

GENERAL INFORMATION: **PRICE: $_____**

Address

Area

Directions

Style   Square feet

Bedrooms and bathrooms   Lot size

Fireplace   Fence or wall

Construction type   Garage

Year built   County

Type of roof   Zoning

Type of heat   Taxes

Security system   Homeowners' dues

ROOM DIMENSIONS AND FLOOR LAYOUT

REMARKS (A more detailed description of the residence may be included. Inclusions and exclusions may be listed here.)

ADDITIONAL INFORMATION:

School District   **Utility Costs**
Elementary   Electricity and Gas
Middle/Junior High   Water and sewer district
High school   Waste management district

Legal and Financial   **Map of the Local Area**
Legal (lot number, etc.)   May highlight local schools
Financing (type)

Listing Agent
Name and address of real estate company
Name of listing agent
Office and mobile telephone numbers

Photograph of House
Exterior
Some interior areas may be included

Track Financial Issues

It's important to keep track of where your money is going when you are moving, especially if you need the proceeds from one home sale to close on another house. Most of the figures for the following charts can be found on your monthly mortgage statement, on your yearly tax bill, from your good faith estimate, or by contacting your real estate agent or relocation counselor. I like to obtain estimates of what these costs will be ahead of time so that I know what price house I can afford to buy next. Then I insert the actual figures into these charts as they become firm.

I don't like surprises when it comes to money, especially at such an emotional time in the moving process as when I am trying to sell my current home and buy a new home. These worktables will provide an accurate record of how much money you will receive at the close of escrow, how much money you will need to close on the sale of your new house, and how many fees and allowances the relocation company will reimburse.

Calculate House Equity on Sale of Current Home

	Estimate	Actual
House sale price	$ _____	$ _____
Less mortgage balance	$ _____	$ _____
Plus/less prorated taxes due	$ _____	$ _____
Plus/less homeowners' fees due	$ _____	$ _____
Less loaned funds (from the relocation company)	$ _____	$ _____
Less Realtor's fees	$ _____	$ _____
Plus/less miscellaneous fees	$ _____	$ _____
Total house equity amount	$ _____	$ _____

Calculate Closing Funds on Purchase of New Home

	Estimate	Actual
Total closing fees (from good faith estimate sheet)	$ _____	$ _____
Less initial deposit on house	$ _____	$ _____
Less additional deposit on house	$ _____	$ _____
Total funds needed at closing	$ _____	$ _____

Calculate Items to Be Reimbursed by Relocation Company

In many corporate relocations, the following fees *may* be reimbursable by your company once you submit your final settlement statement, and any required receipts, to the relocation company. Below is a list of typical fees.

	Estimate	Actual
Realtor's fees	$ _____	$ _____
Attorney's fees	$ _____	$ _____
Closing costs and points*	$ _____	$ _____
Inspection fees*	$ _____	$ _____
House selling allowance*	$ _____	$ _____
Mortgage allowance*	$ _____	$ _____
Day of move expenses (airfare, auto rental, taxi, hotel, and meals)	$ _____	$ _____
Total reimbursable items	$ _____	$ _____

* For tax purposes, these items may be taxed or tax assisted prior to reimbursement.

CHAPTER FOUR

Corporate Relocations

If you are moving as a result of a corporate transfer, consider yourself fortunate. In many of these moves, the relocation company may buy your house if your house does not sell within a specific period of time. Selling your home will then become the responsibility of the relocation company after you move out.

If you fall into this category, it is wise to help the appraiser determine the highest value for your home. You can accomplish this by knowing exactly what to expect when the appraiser arrives at your door. The information in this chapter will help you prepare in advance. The appraiser will take pictures of the inside and outside of your home, so schedule time to get it in shipshape condition to show it at its best! The results of the appraisal will help you decide if you should accept the company buyout offer or continue to sell the house on your own.

As you read this chapter, refer to the Comprehensive Moving Checklist in Appendix A for relocation policy issues.

The Corporate Relocation Appraisal

In many corporate relocations, the company will buy your house if your house does not sell within a specified period of time (usually 90 days). However, before a bona fide offer can be presented to you, a relocation appraisal will have to be completed.

Once the appraisal is completed, you will then have the option of accepting the appraised value or selling the house yourself. The company buyout offer that results from this appraisal process will have a validity period. You must accept or decline this offer, in writing on the applicable form, by the specified deadline.

What Is a Relocation Appraisal?

A relocation appraisal is a highly educated estimate of the most probable sales price at which your home will sell in the current market within a reasonable length of time based on market data (sales comparisons of houses of similar value in your community).

The appraiser will inspect your home and property, analyze the factors that influence the market in your area, and estimate a market value for your home. Since market conditions and housing prices fluctuate over time, this appraised price will be valid only for a specific period of time. The appraiser will then write a professional appraisal report and present it to you or to your relocation company for review.

The Appraisal Process

1. To provide the best market value for your home, obtain at least two appraisals of your home.

2. Sometimes an average of two or more appraised values is used to determine the final offer price to you.

3. An additional appraisal may be necessary if there is significant discrepancy between the first two appraisals.

4. The relocation company will provide a list of appraisers belonging to nationally recognized professional appraisal associations and holding professional membership designations.

5. You can choose two appraisers from this list and also get advice from your real estate agent as to which appraisers he or she would recommend.

6. To obtain a free copy of the Appraisal Institute's National Directory of Members, its education and publication catalogs, or additional information on membership, contact the Appraisal Institute, 875 North Michigan Avenue, Suite 2400, Chicago, IL 60611-1980; (312) 335–4100.

7. The report will be presented to you or to the relocation company. If the report is presented to the relocation company, a copy will be sent to you.

8. Review the report to make sure you agree with the final analysis.

9. The relocation company will then present a bona fide offer to buy your house based on these appraisals.

10. You must accept or decline this offer by a specified date.

How to Help the Appraiser

By having on hand the following additional information and records, you can help the appraiser arrive at the most accurate sales price for your home.

- A plat plan or survey of the house and land.

- A copy of your house blueprints, if available. The appraiser can take measurements from these plans instead of measuring every room and the outside of the house and property. This will save a lot of time.

- A copy of your homeowners' association manual, if applicable, and a statement showing the amount of your monthly homeowners' dues.

- Your property deed, which contains a legal description of the property.

- Your most recent real estate (property) tax bill.

- The Realtor's sales sheet or brochure.

- A factual record of recent sales and listings in the neighborhood, which can be verified by the appraiser. Ask your real estate agent to provide this list.

- Your title policy describing any encroachments.

- A list of personal property to be sold with the house, if any.

- A "brag sheet" listing major home improvements made since you bought the house, the date of installation, and their costs.

- A list of house amenities and appointments that highlights the exceptional qualities of your home.

Hiring a Professional Relocation Expert

If you don't have the time or energy to handle your relocation alone, there are people available to assist with the intricacies of your move. To find a relocation expert, look in the yellow pages of your telephone directory under Relocation Services, ask your real estate agent for a referral, get a recommendation from a friend, or search the Internet. Independent relocation companies are staffed with experienced professionals ready to assist in planning a comprehensive relocation package. They are there to pamper you and provide answers to all of your questions.

Relocation companies are excellent at assisting in the following areas:

- Conducting interviews to determine your family's lifestyle

- Evaluating your relocation requirements and personal desires

- Putting together a package of resources to meet your personal requirements

- Recommending the best real estate agents, moving companies, escrow agents, lenders, insurance agents, inspection companies, appraisers, etc., for your needs

- Helping to get your house ready for sale, assisting in marketing your house, and providing advice when negotiating the final sale

- Locating housing, schools, medical facilities, shopping locations, and recreation facilities in your new community

Hiring a Design Professional

To locate a design professional, look in the yellow pages of your telephone directory under Interior Designers and Decorators, search the Internet, ask your relocation consultant for a referral, or talk to family members and friends and ask for a recommendation. You may also choose to work with the interior designer at your local fine furniture store. It is important to choose a designer whose style and personality are compatible with yours. To ensure that your designer is qualified in the business, make sure he or she is a member of the International Interior Design Association (IIDA) or the American Society of Interior Designers (ASID). You can reach IIDA at (888) 799–4432 or www.iida.com. Call ASID's free worldwide referral service at (800) 775–2743 or visit www.interiors.org.

Many designers will come to your home and provide a free initial consultation. They can help you create and implement a design plan. They can also help you purchase furniture, window coverings, floor coverings, accessories, and other products that are available to the design community through special showrooms not open to the public.

CHAPTER FIVE

The Quest for the Perfect Home

Whether you are buying or renting, finding a new place to live takes time and patience. It also requires that you do your homework in advance so you know what you are looking for and what you can afford. If you are moving to a new area of the country that you are completely unfamiliar with, you may choose to rent until you get a better feel for the area. Alternatively, if you take one or two house-hunting trips, and are prepared ahead of time, you will be more successful in locating and purchasing the home of your choice quickly.

Begin your homework by filling out the forms included in this chapter. If you can articulate to your real estate agent in precise terms the type of home you are looking for, you will not waste time on homes that won't appeal to you. It's also important to apply for a loan prequalification letter from your lender before you start house hunting. In today's competitive real estate market, eager buyers submit a prequalification letter with an offer to demonstrate that they are qualified to purchase a home of a certain value.

I used this chapter's forms for my last three moves, and they helped me to purchase a house on my initial or second house-hunting trip. Remember to bring a blank check when you leave on your house-hunting trip so that you can leave a deposit when you make an offer on a new home. Good luck in your quest for the perfect home!

Review a Map of the Area

If you are moving to a new area, obtain a map of the entire area. Review the map to make sure you are buying a house in the part of town where you will be most content. Envision your life in the new city. Think about distances to places that you will frequent the most, location of freeways, areas of traffic congestion, and routes and distances to your workplace and to the airport.

At the same time that you are evaluating the house and the specific neighborhood in which you are planning to buy, evaluate the area within a 5-mile radius of where you will spend most of your time. Drive or walk around in this area to make sure that it suits your lifestyle. Then drive around the area adjoining your prospective new neighborhood. Check out the distances to the local supermarkets, cleaners, drugstore, schools, gas stations, movie rental stores, health clubs, etc.

As you are driving around, take note of amenities in the area like sidewalks, crosswalks, bike paths, landscaped public areas, community parks, and streetlights. Check the access in and out of the neighborhood. Ask yourself these types of questions before purchasing your new home: Is there a traffic light at the junction of a busy highway that enables you to enter and exit the neighborhood quickly and safely? Is the neighborhood a safe place for children to ride bikes and play? Is the commute to work manageable? Do you feel at home in this new area?

Decide Which House to Buy

Your real estate agent will be able to find you a house more rapidly if he or she knows what type of house and neighborhood most interest you. If you get the entire family to participate in the search to find a new home, you will experience more cooperation during the move and will find the perfect home more quickly.

Using the following form, ask each person in the family to write down a wish list of what he or she wants in the new house. List each item in order of importance, the first being the most important. Even though you will not be able to satisfy all of the requirements of every person, make sure that each person gets a few wish list features. The entire family will benefit enormously if each member has something to gain from the move.

Your New House Wish List

_____   _____

_____   _____

_____   _____

_____   _____

_____   _____

_____   _____

_____   _____

_____   _____

_____   _____

Once you've narrowed down your selection of homes or apartments, evaluate your top two choices to weigh the positive and negative aspects of each location. Consider price, location, school district, floor plan, quality, and emotional appeal when making this list. This information will provide the framework to properly evaluate which house to finally select.

First Option	**Second Option**
_____	_____
_____	_____
_____	_____
_____	_____
_____	_____
_____	_____
_____	_____
_____	_____

Martha's Moving Survival Tips

Not on a map. New housing developments pose interesting problems. The express delivery company told me that it could not locate our new house on the local map. Since we were the second house to be occupied in this development, the situation was understandable. But I still needed my package! So I gave the company specific directions to my house, and a courier delivered my package the following day. There haven't been problems locating our house since.

The Mortgage Application Process

Unless you are financially wealthy, you will need a loan to purchase your new home. Even if you have been through this process before, you may want to organize the specific paperwork required to process your mortgage application ahead of time.

Prequalify for a Loan

Your real estate agent needs to know your financial status to determine your housing price range. The strongest buyers secure financing before submitting a contract on a home. This is called prequalifying. Prequalifying lets you know exactly how much money you are qualified to borrow. Obtain a formal prequalification letter from your lender. Many real estate agencies and relocation companies have relationships with lending partners to help you through this process. These types of companies can assist you with many services, including finding a new house and providing a lender. You may also be eligible to receive savings on closing costs associated with your mortgage when using this type of company.

Online Mortgage Approvals

A group of pioneer lenders and loan brokers operating on the Internet are using computer programs to customize mortgages for individual home buyers. Three such sites include www.priceline.com, www.indymacbank.com, and www.home advisor.msn.com. You can search the Web for other lenders offering the same type of online service. These futuristic lenders combine automated underwriting, credit scores, and other factors including location, the amount of property taxes on the house, whether it is a primary or secondary residence, and whether the borrower is a potential repeat customer. With this type of program, if you are considered a good credit risk, you may qualify for a lower interest rate than what is offered by "prime" or "sub-prime" lenders.

Using a proprietary automated underwriting system, these online services can provide real-time credit decisions by the time consumers have finished completing the online application. The application takes about fifteen minutes to complete online, and then there will be a follow-up phone call from a loan adviser to complete the transaction. Rates and fees for this service are typically lower than through a traditional lender because there is greater efficiency and less overhead in a Web-based operation.

The Paperwork Trail

Online or on paper, a mortgage application requires a lot of detailed information. The lender can help in this process by drawing a clear picture of your financial status. However, to do this, the lender will need detailed paperwork that documents your employment status, marital status, and net worth. Your net worth is determined by your assets (your property, holdings, and possessions) minus your liabilities (what you owe). Most lenders will require the following information:

- **Tax information.** Provide a copy of your W-2s and your income tax returns (Schedule 1040), including all schedules for the last two years.

- **Home addresses.** Provide a list of your residences for the previous two to ten years, depending on the lender's requirements.

- **Employment information.** Provide a list of your employers for the last two to ten years, depending on the lender's requirements. Provide each employer's name, address, phone number, and list your dates of employment and gross monthly income.

- **Income.** Indicate salary, overtime, bonuses, commissions, dividends, interest, retirement, Social Security, or any other source of ongoing income. A copy of your two most recent paychecks may also be required.

- **Social Security numbers.** Include the numbers of both the borrower and coborrower on the loan.

- **Source(s) of cash deposit.** Amount for the down payment and where held.

- **Real estate owned.** Include property address, estimated market value of all property currently owned, and the balance and payments on all outstanding mortgages. Provide a copy of your most recent mortgage statement, or provide the name, address, phone number, and account number of the mortgage company holding the loan. Include documentation for any outstanding liens, rental income, mortgage payments, taxes, insurance policy, and homeowners' and maintenance dues.

■ **Other assets:**

Automobiles (owned or leased). Year, model, value, and a copy of the loan balance due on your motor vehicle(s). If you own the vehicle(s) free and clear, a copy of the title will be required. The current value of your vehicle can be found in the *Kelly Blue Book*, online at www.kbb.com, or in hard copy at your local AAA office or at the library.

Life insurance policy. Face amount, monthly premiums, and cash value of your life insurance policy. If the cash value is to be used as a portion of your down payment and/or closing costs, documentation from the insurance company of the present cash value may be required.

Investments. Details of investments owned (stocks, bonds, IRA accounts, etc.). A copy of the last two statements for your account(s) may be required.

Retirement fund. Include vested interest in a retirement fund. A copy of the investment statement(s) may be required.

Business owned. The net worth of any business owned. A copy of your financial statement(s) may be required.

Personal Property. The current value of all personal property owned. (Refer to inventory checklist in Chapter Two to estimate the value of your personal property.)

■ **Liquid assets.** Bank, savings and loan, or credit union names, addresses, account numbers, and balances for all checking and savings accounts. A copy of the last two statements may be required.

■ **Liabilities.** Creditor names, account numbers, and outstanding balances for all liabilities including:

Alimony	401K loans
Child support	Stock pledges
Credit card debt	Student loans
Automobile loans	Other real estate mortgages
Bank loans	Home equity loans
Credit union loans	Margin account loans
Cosigned loans	Personal business loans
Life insurance loans	Other liabilities
Notes payable	

■ **Divorce decrees.** If you or your spouse has ever been divorced, copies of all applicable divorce decrees may be required. However, alimony, child support, or separate maintenance income need be revealed only if the borrower or coborrower chooses to have it considered for repayment of the loan.

■ **Loan application form.** To obtain loan approval as quickly as possible:

1. Fill out the loan application form completely and accurately.
2. Attach copies of all required documentation.
3. Sign the application form (both borrower and coborrower) in all designated places.
4. Make copies for yourself before mailing.
5. Include a check if a loan-processing fee is required in advance.

■ **Appraisal contact.** Provide the name and phone number of the person to contact to schedule and gain access to the contract property for the loan appraisal.

Compare Mortgages

Finding the loan that is right for you may take some research. Every person has a different financial picture and every lender has different mortgage packages with varying rates and terms. Before your loan rate can be locked in, you will need to fill out the lender's application form and pay an application fee.

I use the following chart to compare my choices after I have narrowed my research down to three lenders. Carefully evaluate all terms of the agreement as well as the loan rate. You may want to evaluate the lending institution itself: Is the company financially stable, and are you satisfied with the level of customer service provided?

On the purchase of our most recent house, I decided to use the Internet to find a loan. I enjoyed the convenience of locating information on my own schedule. It was great to be able to narrow down my choices quickly and efficiently, instead of having to wait for someone to call me back on the phone. I did contact a few lenders recommended by my relocation company, but they could not match the rates offered over the Internet. Indy Mac Bank was my final choice because of its professionalism, rate options, and terms, and its willingness to meet my quick closing date.

Be sure to refer to the Comprehensive Moving Checklist in Appendix A for banking and financial issues regarding your move.

Mortgage Rate Comparison Chart

Property address/lot number _____

Purchase price $ _____

Loan product (type of dwelling) _____

Loan amount $ _____

Down payment (_____ %) $ _____

Purpose: Purchase   Refinance (Circle one)

Occupancy type: Owner-occupied   Second home Investment (Circle one)

	First quote	Second quote	Third quote
Mortgage company	_____	_____	_____
Lender's name	_____	_____	_____
Contact phone number	_____	_____	_____

Loan type: conventional, jumbo (usually over $250K), FHA*, VA** (Circle one)

Fixed rate:	First quote	Second quote	Third quote
15 year	_____	_____	_____
30 year	_____	_____	_____
Adjustable rate:			
6 months	_____	_____	_____
1 year	_____	_____	_____
3 years	_____	_____	_____
5 years	_____	_____	_____
7 years	_____	_____	_____
Graduated payment:	_____	_____	_____
Balloon payment:	_____	_____	_____
Loan payments:			
Monthly	_____	_____	_____
Bimonthly	_____	_____	_____
Origination fee:			
(Up to __ % of loan amount)	_____	_____	_____
Discount points:			
(Up to __ % of loan amount)	_____	_____	_____
Rate expiration date:	_____	_____	_____

* Federal Housing Administration   ** Veterans Administration

Guidelines for Finding a New School

Since all children have different needs, there are all types of schools available to meet these needs. Today's options include public schools, private schools, religious schools, home schooling, and boarding schools. Gifted and talented programs are designed to help children learn at an accelerated pace. There are also programs available for children requiring special assistance.

To find schools in your area, look in the yellow pages of your telephone directory for school listings or search on the Internet. For comprehensive listings, visit your local library or bookstore to find publications that detail the public and private schools in your state. These guides are excellent sources for starting your search. However, there is no substitute for visiting the school and talking directly with the principal and the teachers. Also talk to other parents who have schoolchildren. Ask them which school district is considered to be the best in the area or what they have heard about a particular school's reputation. Schools are a hot topic today, and most people will talk endlessly about education. Valuable information can be gathered by speaking with people at your local park, community center, church, or library.

Publications about public schools are usually organized by school district. They are full of useful information, such as mission statement, learning environment, special programs and unique features, foreign languages, special education programs, behavior management strategies, teacher support, class size, calendar year, parent involvement, athletic programs, student assessment, and honors and awards for the school or teachers.

Publications about private schools are usually listed in alphabetical order. They contain information about accreditation, principal, contact person, date founded, grades, enrollment, dress code, costs, services, student profile, admission requirements, curriculum, parent involvement, teaching approach, scholarships available, facilities, and services.

Martha's Moving Survival Tips

Public schools are not always free. In some states, public schools charge tuition to students not yet residing in the district, even though the parents have signed a contract to buy a house in the district. Students can be charged tuition from their start date at the school until the house closing date. Sometimes this tuition is waived at the board of education's discretion. Inquire about the policy of your new school district, and find out in advance how much tuition you may be required to pay.

The Internet and your real estate agent are great resources to locate comprehensive reports on most school districts in the United States. Two popular Web sites include the School Report at www.theschoolreport.com and School Match at www.schoolmatch.com.

Look in the local newspaper for seminars on choosing the right school for your child and for private school open houses. Whichever school you choose, both child and parents should be happy with the decision. It is crucial that children and parents work together in the education process to make sure each child's learning experience is productive.

Be sure to refer to the school section of the Comprehensive Moving Checklist, too.

Questions to Ask When Evaluating a New School

1. What are the school hours?
2. When does the school year start and end?
3. How do students get to school?
4. How many students are in a classroom?
5. How many students are in the school?
6. What grades are included in the school?
7. What standard curriculum is offered?
8. How many hours of homework are expected per night?
9. Is there a list of materials that I will need to provide?
10. What will my child's daily schedule be like?
11. How are the students graded?
12. How many report cards are distributed per year?
13. What standard achievement tests will be given?
14. Does the school have a gifted and talented program?
15. Does the school have a special education program?
16. How are special students integrated into the classroom?
17. When are parent-teacher conferences?
18. How should I contact you if I have a question?
    E-mail? _____   Phone? _____   Write a note? _____
    Stop by in the morning or after school? _____

19. Does the school have a full-time librarian?

20. Does the school have a full-time guidance counselor?

21. Does the school have a computer lab?
    How many students per computer?
    Does the school have a dedicated computer teacher?

22. How many recesses do students have per day?

23. Does the school offer a foreign language program?
    In what grade does this program start?
    What languages are offered?

24. Does the school have an art program?
    Is there a dedicated art room and art teacher?

25. Does the school have a gymnasium?
    How many days per week do students have gym?

26. Does the school have an instrument program?
    In what grade does this program start?
    What instruments are offered?
    Is there an instrument rental or purchase program?
    Are instrument music lessons offered during school?
    Is there a charge for lessons?
    If yes, how much per hour?

27. Does the school have a band or orchestra?
    When does it practice?

28. Does the school have a choir?
    At what grade does this program start?
    Do students have to try out?
    When do they practice?
    Do they wear a choir uniform?

29. Is there a school theatrical performance?
    Do students have to try out?
    When do they practice?
    When and where are performances held?

30. Does the school sponsor a Boy or Girl Scout program?

31. Does the school sponsor a student council program?

32. Is there a before- and after-school child-care program?
    If yes, what are the hours of operation?

33. Are there any special after-school programs or clubs?

34. Does the school have a National Honor Society?

35. Does the school hold awards assemblies?

36. Does the school offer competitive sports programs?

37. Does the school have a full-time nurse?

38. Does the school have a hot lunch program?
     How many days of the week is hot lunch provided?
     Is there a milk program?
     Can snacks be purchased?
     Where do the students eat lunch?

39. Are the bathrooms inside or outside?
     Do the bathrooms have doors on the stalls?

40. How do parents participate in the school?

41. How do parents participate in the classroom?

42. How is security handled?

43. Is there a full-time police officer on duty at the school?

44. Are drugs and alcohol a problem on campus?

45. How is discipline handled?

46. Does the school have a dress code?
     Are uniforms required or certain clothes restricted?

47. How will additions to the school be planned and funded?

48. Is there adequate parking for students and visitors?

49. Is tuition charged for out-of-district students?

50. If a private school, is there a waiting list to get in?

51. Is financial aid available?

Web Sites Providing Relocation Information

The Internet is becoming a major resource for those contemplating a move. Many relocation specialists are increasingly making their services available via the Internet. Government agencies post information relevant to services.

1. State, city, and municipal government Web sites can provide the following information:
   - General information about the economy, state services, and office locations
   - Driver's license requirements, vehicle taxes, and vehicle registration
   - Property, sales, and income tax details
   - School information such as faculty, curriculum, registration requirements, test scores, academic calendars, and neighborhood boundaries

2. The Web site at www.homestore.com provides relocation information not included in this moving guide, such as city reports, school reports, home listings, community information, tools and calculators, consumer information, and special offers. A salary calculator can estimate the income needed at a new destination to replicate your current lifestyle. You can also locate a real estate agent in your neighborhood on this site.

3. Yahoo has a Real Estate page at www.yahoo.com where you can select two cities and compare them by cost of living, real estate prices, quality of life, climate, etc. You can also find a salary comparison from city to city.

4. Relocation Mall at www.relomall.com helps users find apartments and roommates, rent furniture, and locate sources for packing boxes, movers, and storage facilities.

5. If you need assistance moving your automobile, pets, or any large household items from and to any of the fifty states, log on to www.autorelo.com.

6. Locating decorating information online is easy today. Two popular sites that may be helpful in your search are www.homeportfolio.com and www.decoratorsecrets.com.

7. To pay government taxes and fees, property taxes, parking tickets, and moving violation fees, log on to www.officialpayments.com.

8. The Social Security Administration can be reached by calling (800) 772–1213 or by going to www.ssa.gov.

9. The Internal Revenue Service can be reached at (800) 829–1040 or on its Web site at www.irs.ustreas.gov.

10. Monster Moving at www.monstermoving.com can help you find a mover, change your address online, connect or disconnect your utilities online, get a free mortgage quote, get a city profile report, etc.

11. Many real estate agents now provide virtual tours of homes online. Most of these tours are uploaded onto www.realtor.com and www.homeadvisor.msn.com. The tours provide 360-degree views of a house and usually include as many as eight scenes of the house and property. Agents are using such marketing tools more aggressively today, especially for high-end homes.

12. To locate specific neighborhood demographic details, go to www.homeadvisor.msn.com. Under the heading Find Houses for Sale, click on Neighborhoods. Then enter a specific zip code.

Practical Tips for Buying a House and Relocation in General

Here are a few practical tips I have gathered through the years regarding purchasing a house and relocation in general. These are not hard-and-fast rules but guidelines to help in your buying decision and the relocation process in general.

- When buying a house, think "location, location, location" and "resale."

- Buy in a reputable school district, if you can afford to do so, even if you do not have school-age children. A quality house in a well-recognized school district usually has good resale value, and it may sell more quickly.

- If given the choice, move to an area of the country where the economy is strong. Houses tend to appreciate faster in such areas.

- Houses with neutral carpet or tile and neutral-color walls tend to sell faster because they appeal to the largest number of buyers.

- In some areas of the country, houses less than ten years old tend to sell faster then older homes (unless the older homes have been remodeled), because new houses require less maintenance and are usually located in the most desirable areas of town.

- The most expensive house in the neighborhood is sometimes more difficult to sell, unless there is something that makes it more appealing than other houses in the area. If there are less expensive houses on the market at the same time with comparable features, the less expensive houses will usually sell first.

- When moving to a new area of the country, look at houses in several price ranges and in different parts of town. This will give you a better feel for the market in the area. The most expensive house may not always be the best house for your needs. Also remember that the tax laws changed in 1997 and you no longer have to buy a house of equal or greater value to defer paying capital gains on your current property. (Contact your accountant or the IRS for further information on this subject.)

- Timing is everything. If the real estate market is strong in your area, you can usually profit when you sell your house. In most corporate relocations, the company pays the real estate fees and all moving expenses. Therefore, if you make sure your move is cost effective, you may be able to make a handsome profit each time you move. If you're willing to put forth the time and energy, this can be an added bonus to relocation.

- In many cases, one spouse is off pursuing his or her new job and will leave the relocation process to the other spouse, known as the trailing spouse. If you are the trailing spouse, following the advice in this guide will help you immensely during this challenging period in your life. If you think of the move as a full-time job, the transition to your new location will go more smoothly.

- Houses with well-laid-out floor plans usually sell faster than houses with cumbersome floor plans. The kitchen and master bedroom are the two top selling features of a house today.

- Houses with four bedrooms, three bathrooms, and an office are popular in today's market and tend to have the greatest market appeal to families.

Martha's Moving Survival Tips

Rusty metal shelves. I moved to my new house only to discover rusty metal shelves that I did not like nor want in my garage. I called the real estate agent and informed him of my problem. He had the shelves hauled away at his own expense. You can avoid this type of confusion if, at the final walk-through before closing, you tell the agent about items you do not want left in the house. The owners will be instructed to remove them.

■ Houses with superior amenities usually sell faster. (Examples include outstanding views; a master planned community; a lake, park, or golf course nearby; bike paths; mature landscaping; a safe neighborhood; a good school district; historic district; privacy; charm; etc.)

■ When buying a new house, you may have to allocate extra money for upgraded items not included in the list price of the house. Such items may include designer upgrades (tile, carpet, flooring, countertops, appliances, etc.), landscaping, decks, window coverings, built-in shelves, an entertainment center, built-in refrigerator, rain gutters, finished basement, pool, security system, central vacuum, etc. If you want your home to look like the model, work with the designer to incorporate the special touches that make the model unique.

■ Houses priced correctly usually sell faster. If your agent feels that your house is priced too high, it may not sell as quickly as those priced more competitively. Listen to your agent's advice if you do not want your home to be on the market for an extended period of time.

■ If you close on your house during the warmer months of the year and don't plan on moving in for several weeks or longer, make sure that the lawn sprinkler system is set appropriately (if applicable) and that you hire a lawn service to cut your grass during the interim period. You don't want to permanently damage your trees, plants, or grass by neglecting to care for them.

■ Houses located at busy intersections are sometimes more difficult to sell. These areas tend to generate more noise from automobile traffic. In addition, bright lights may shine in the windows at night, depending on the angle of the house.

■ Houses located adjacent to large parks, a community swimming pool, or schools are sometimes more difficult to sell because there may be more traffic, noise, and vandalism in such areas.

■ In certain locations, houses with a septic tank system are sometimes more difficult to sell than houses using the city sewer system. If the neighborhood is planning to have city sewers installed in the future, the new owner may be held financially responsible for the cost of mandatory hookup.

■ Real estate agents do their best to provide up-to-date, accurate information about the area where you will be buying a house. However, it is your responsibility as a consumer to verify that the information they have provided is correct. Agents are only human and sometimes make mistakes, or they do not always have access to the most recent information. Be an informed consumer, instead of trying to blame someone else for a mistake after the fact.

■ Neighborhoods are sometimes divided into two or three separate school districts depending on where the district lines are drawn. It is your responsibility, not your agent's, to make sure you are buying a home in the school district of your choice. The agent cannot be held legally liable if you make a mistake and buy a house on the wrong side of the district's boundary line. (School district boundary lines may change over time. The grade levels in the school may also change from year to year. It is best to call the school yourself to make sure you have the most accurate information.)

■ Every citizen is entitled to know if she is buying or renting in a safe part of town. You can contact the local police station in the area for information regarding any drug problems, robberies, or sex offenders in a neighborhood. The police department will provide this information to you free or for a minimal fee. You can also ask if there are any jails or state prisons in the area, or propositions on the ballot to build any, that could make a neighborhood potentially undesirable in the future.

■ When your house is on the market, always keep your house in ship-shape condition. House showings usually occur when you least expect them.

■ If you move frequently, keep a list of all of your work and residential addresses in your computer database for future reference when filling out application forms.

■ If possible, buy a house on the side of town where you won't drive into the sun on your way to and from work everyday.

■ Even if your new residence is only temporary, unpack your belongings, hang up pictures, and get involved in your new community. It will take motivation and energy on your part to get settled, but the reward is a better quality of life, even if only for a year or two. Remember that children benefit enormously when they feel settled in their new surroundings and are involved in their new community.

CHAPTER SIX

One Month to Go

The countdown continues! You've got one month before you move. What's next? Several things, including getting rid of unwanted or unnecessary belongings, selecting a mover, transferring records, and scheduling and confirming key dates. After reading this chapter, you'll want to refer to the Comprehensive Moving Checklist in Appendix A for more moving details.

Dispose of Unwanted Household Belongings

I considered myself a very organized person until the first time my family moved. I didn't realize how much stuff we had accumulated since my husband and I were married, and I was unprepared on moving day. If I had discarded unnecessary items ahead of time, I would have saved money since we were paying for the move ourselves.

However, I learned from this mistake and never repeated it. I now purge everything that is not necessary before I move. I go through my files and dispose of all obsolete papers, I give unwanted items to charitable organizations, and I throw away anything that is damaged or nonessential. When our children were young they did not want to get rid of their "treasures." I used moving as a method to get rid of things they no longer needed and told them the items were probably lost during the move so that they would not get overly upset about their missing belongings. After the move we would buy something new to replace the missing item, and it became a win-win situation for everyone.

There are several ways to get rid of belongings that you no longer want to keep. A good rule of thumb is that if you have not used an item for a year and do not plan to use it again, get rid of it. Exceptions are items with sentimental value or with intrinsic value, such as antiques. However, the biggest dilemma most people face when trying to get rid of possessions is the psychological attachment to the objects. This section provides systematic ways to help you part with excess "stuff." You may want to combine several of the methods mentioned to reduce your inventory before you move.

Hold a Garage Sale

Advertise in the classified ads section of the newspaper to get a good turnout. Here's an example of an advertisement: "Furniture, Household Items, and Plants for Sale. Saturday, May 6, 8:00 A.M.–6:00 P.M. Cash only. 1 Ocean Drive, San Diego. Call John at 555–1234 for details."

On the day of the sale, put a large, colorful sign (you can also add a few flags or balloons) in front of your house ("Incredible Furniture Moving Sale—Saturday, May 6, 8:00 A.M.–6:00 P.M.") and one or two more signs on a main thoroughfare ("Furniture Moving Sale—2 blocks straight ahead"). Organize your merchandise in an attractive, uncluttered manner. Be prepared to have people show up at your house at 8:00 A.M. Many people travel from sale to sale on weekends and like to get an early start.

Tag each sale item with a price. Set fair and reasonable prices for your merchandise. Buyers like to negotiate to feel that they are getting a bargain. Make it a win-win situation for you and the buyer. Be prepared to get a low bid on the first offer. Then try to negotiate a higher price for the item. Hold firm in your asking price early in the day. Let customers know that you may lower the price at the end of the day if the item has not sold, but that you will only hold an item for a specified time limit, say thirty minutes. If another buyer comes along after the time limit, you will sell the item.

Be firm and take cash only (unless a familiar neighbor or a friend is buying the item). This will guard against the problem of getting bad checks. Have plenty of cash on hand to make change for large bills, and keep it in a protected place. Post a sign stating that all sales are final.

Donate Items to Charitable Organizations

Your extra and unwanted belongings may be appreciated by the needy. Consider donating to the Salvation Army, Goodwill Industries of America (or of your city),

St. Vincent de Paul Society, Disabled American Veterans, or your local church or school. Check your municipal Web site for special county collection days.

Always request a receipt for tax purposes. Charitable organizations are usually listed in the business section of the white pages in your local phone book. Charities will often send out a truck to pick up large items. Goodwill and Salvation Army have donation drop boxes for smaller items; call for directions to your nearest drop-off location and ask for a list of items they take. Different organizations have different requirements for what they will accept. You may need to work with more than one organization to dispose of all of your unwanted items. *Caution:* If you donate your computer, first erase the hard drive to delete all personal information from your computer to avoid the possibility of identity theft.

Donate Books to the Library and Old Eyeglasses to the Needy

Ask your local library staff if they accept books. Donated books are either added to the library's circulating collection or sold at a library book sale, which funds library programs and special events. Various eye-care organizations can revive your old glasses for the needy.

Sell or Recycle Unwanted Appliances

Advertise in the newspaper to sell working appliances. Or call a local dealer to get rid of unwanted refrigerators, washers, dryers, and stoves. Check your municipal Web site for county or town collection days.

Call an Auction House or an Appraiser

An auction house can appraise and potentially buy expensive furniture, artwork, fur coats, etc. You can also call an appraiser to have high-value items appraised for insurance purposes. (Keep appraisal documents in your possession during your move.) Auction houses and appraisers are listed in the yellow pages of your phone directory or on the Internet.

Sell on the Internet

EBay is like an international electronic auction house. Sellers can log on to www.ebay.com to post items, then buyers put in a bid price for the items they are interested in buying. EBay runs the Web service and collects a token listing fee plus a commission ranging from 1.25 to 5 percent anytime a sale is completed. A clever system helps to cut down on dishonest transactions. Since sellers rarely meet face-to-face and most of the merchandise sold is mailed to the buyer, sellers can share feedback on the Web site to alert others about dishonest buyers. Even though the site management provides the feedback forum, eBay takes no responsibility for transactions that do not go through.

Caveat emptor (buyer beware): If you send someone money but you never receive the merchandise, eBay cannot be held financially responsible.

Amazon and Yahoo have similar types of auction services. Visit www .amazon.com or www.yahoo.com, then click on Auctions to buy or sell an item.

Confirm Your House Closing and Move-In Date

Confirm with your real estate agent your house closing date (or both dates if you are buying and selling simultaneously). Do this *before* scheduling your final moving date. You must sign all required closing documents before you receive the house

---

The Empty Nester's Guide to Flying the Coop

Are you an empty nester planning to make a move? If so, consider how much space you actually need. Do you really want your new home cluttered with stuff you don't want or will never use again? Now is the time to pare down so that everything will fit in your lovely new home. Review the following list of ways to part more easily with years of accumulated possessions. Get started today and be free of the clutter and flush with cash.

- Start with any children's belongings remaining at the house. Be firm in telling your children that their "treasures" will be properly disposed of if not removed by a certain date. If your children have moved to another town, ask them to go through their belongings on the next visit home.

- Pass along antiques and valuable items to family members who will appreciate them, or sell them if there is no one who wants them.

- Get rid of duplicate dishes, glasses, and worn-out sheets and bedding.

- Sell things that you will not use after you move, such as extra bedroom furniture, an old television set, a lawn mower, and a snowblower.

- Live by the saying "When in doubt, throw it out." This applies to sentimental items. Take a photo of the object you want to remember and then throw or give away the actual item.

keys. Therefore, it's best to schedule your move-in date for the day after closing to give the movers an entire day to unload the truck. If you will be renting, reconfirm your move-in date.

If possible, do not schedule your house-selling and house-buying closing dates on the same day. If the house-selling closing slips, it will impact your house-buying closing date and could jeopardize the terms of your contract, resulting in additional fees.

If you are moving long-distance, it's best to schedule your house-buying and house-selling dates three to four days apart to ensure a smooth closing on both ends of the transaction. Since a long-distance moving van will be in transit with your belongings from several days to a week, coordinating house closings on two different dates becomes simpler. Be sure to call your lender to confirm that the loan for the new house has been approved.

Choose Your Moving Option

If your move is not the result of a corporate relocation, one of the biggest decisions you will make about the move is whether to hire a moving company to do the entire job, do the entire job yourself, or choose a combination of the two. You basically have four choices depending on how much money you want to pay and how much time you want to spend on your move. There are advantages and disadvantages in each of the following scenarios. I recommend options one and two only to people with very few belongings, to the young and the strong, or to those folks with several good, strong friends.

Option One: Do the entire job yourself. Rent or borrow a truck and pack and move all of your own boxes.

Option Two: You pack and load the trailer and a moving company drives it to your home. Then you unload and unpack.

Option Three: Pack your own boxes, hire someone to load and unload and drive the truck, and then unpack yourself.

Option Four: Hire a moving company to do the entire job, including the packing, loading, moving, unloading, and sometimes the unpacking too.

For corporate transfers, relocation companies are authorized to provide different levels of relocation services depending on the job title you hold at your company. As you move up the corporate ranks, you may be entitled to a higher level of service each time you move. This benefit can be an added incentive to transferees and their families, who may have to move several times during their careers.

Get a Moving Bid or Schedule Moving Help

After your house has sold, you will get many phone calls from moving van lines offering to provide a free moving bid. If you have not committed to a moving company yet, I recommend that you get at least three moving bids. Find moving companies in your phone book, choose three movers who have contacted you, or get recommendations from neighbors, friends, or relatives. Alternatively, you can go to www.monstermoving.com for smart ideas on choosing a moving company.

Each moving company will send a representative to your house or apartment to provide a free quote. In making your final decision, you may not always want to choose the lowest bidder. You may want to consider a mover's reputation in the industry, its availability, and its responsiveness to your needs.

If you are moving yourself, reserve a rental truck or make plans to borrow a truck from a friend or relative. Politely ask your family or friends for help with your move. Schedule a moving party. Provide food and beverages to entice people to help you. Alternatively, you may choose to hire a local moving company that will provide moving help at an hourly rate. You can also hire movers to pack your boxes, or you can pack all the boxes yourself

Once you make your final selection, get a written estimate and follow these steps:

1. Ask the moving company for a written estimate that is binding and guaranteed not to exceed a certain amount. Note that there may be extra charges imposed for additional services (see step 4 below) if the services are not brought to the moving company's attention at the time the estimate is completed. You will also want to discuss crating services, specialty services, high-value items and high-value inventory, insurance requirements, the moving date, and the location and distance to the new residence. Find out if the insurance coverage is based on the original price of the item or replacement value. Replacement value is usually preferred. Refer to the checklist in Appendix A for a complete list of details to discuss with the moving company.

2. Obtain each company's assigned motor carrier number and call the U.S. Department of Transportation at (202) 358–7000 to determine if the company is registered and has the proper insurance on file.

3. Ask the moving company for a copy of the free booklet *Your Rights and Responsibilities When You Move.*

4. Discuss in advance the fees for "additional services" (such as an extra flight of steps, a long carry, and crated items). This is the only way you can prevent the moving company from changing the price or terms of the contract without legal recourse on your part.

5. Request unpacking services at this time.

Schedule Your Moving Date

Schedule your moving date and make sure you get this date commitment in writing. From June through September, it is more difficult to get your requested moving date. Many people move in the summer to accommodate their children's school schedules and to take advantage of good weather. Schedule your moving date thirty to sixty days in advance to reserve your slot during this busy time of year.

If you are not in a hurry to move, you may want to schedule your move between October and May to save money. Some moving companies discount moving rates in this off-season. In addition, off-season moving personnel tend to be more professional. Since the summer is the peak moving time, moving companies have to hire seasonal workers to accommodate demand. These temporary workers are not always as experienced as the full-time staff.

Martha's Moving Survival Tips

Movers are not mountain men. If you are moving into a property with a steep driveway, the moving company will usually rent a smaller truck or van to shuttle the furniture and boxes up the hill so that the movers don't get overly fatigued going up and down the hill. However, if your furniture is being delivered on a Sunday, all of the truck rental agencies can be closed.

When my movers came to me with this problem, I immediately told them to use my van. They said that it was against company rules to use the owner's vehicle because they would not be insured for damage. I told them that my automobile insurance policy would cover any damage, and they immediately jumped at the option of using the van. It saved them at least four extra hours of backbreaking work.

Remember that the movers are only human. Treat movers with respect, and they will repay you in kind by being extra careful with your belongings.

Martha's Moving Survival Tips

Another computer glitch. If you are moving into a brand-new residential neighborhood, your new house may not be listed in the cable company's computer database. Don't panic! After the cable company receives your initial call, it will input your new address into their computer system. It may take a few days to a week before your address is activated in the system. Once it is in the database, you will be able to schedule hookup service. There's a simple way to avoid this glitch: Call your cable company several weeks ahead of your move-in date.

Obtain Utility Company Numbers and Requirements

Obtain names, phone numbers, and requirements (such as deposits and connection requirements) for utility companies. Your real estate agent can usually provide this information to you, or you can look it up in a local telephone directory. Refer to the worksheets in Appendix B for details about connecting and disconnecting utilities.

Transfer School Records

Request a records transfer form and a registration form from the new school your child will be attending. Fill in the registration form and return it promptly to the front office. To expedite the transfer of records, hand deliver the records transfer form (completely and accurately filled out) to the school administration office in your current school. The school will then forward all requested information to the new school.

Schedule Final Doctor and Dentist Appointments

If you have medical issues to discuss or resolve with your current physician or dentist, schedule a final appointment well in advance of your moving date. The staff in your current doctor's office may be able to recommend a doctor in your new community if they have contacts in that area.

Notify Organizations and People of Your Move

Start sending out letters of notification of your move to organizations, clubs, and people listed in the Comprehensive Moving Checklist (see Appendix A) as soon as possible.

Transfer or Cancel Club Memberships

If you are moving out of town, remember to cancel or transfer your club memberships. Fill out any required paperwork to initiate this process and make sure you receive any refunds owed.

Cancel Charge Accounts

If you are moving out of town, cancel charge accounts at local stores. Reapply for local store charge accounts and discount grocery store cards after you move. If you are planning to change banks, apply for new ATM bankcards.

Schedule Pickup of Rented Items

If you have a piano or any other large item that is being rented, schedule a date and time for pickup by the rental company. Keep receipts for all returned items in case of a dispute. Refer to the checklist in Appendix A for details.

Martha's Moving Survival Tips

Don't leave your mail in limbo. If there will be a gap in time between moving out of your current home and moving into your new one, don't forget to send the post office an authorization-to-hold-mail form in addition to a change-of-address form. Both forms can be filled out and returned to the post office together. Your mail will be held at the post office in your new location. Depending on how much mail you have accumulated and the rules governing the post office in your area, your mail may be delivered to your door in a box, or you may have to go to the post office and pick up the mail yourself. If your mail has not been delivered on the day requested, call your local post office immediately and ask if you need to retrieve it.

Schedule Your Automobile for Service

If you will be driving long-distance to your new location, schedule a service checkup for your automobile. It could be an agonizing experience if your automobile broke down during your trip. If you have an emergency road service provider, make sure your identification card has not expired. You won't want to be denied service if an emergency arises.

Schedule Your Going-Away Party

Refer to Chapter One for details.

Cancel Home Services

Home services are items or services delivered to your home on a daily, weekly, or monthly basis—such as newspaper delivery, dry-cleaning service, and pest extermination service. Home services include services provided to maintain your home, such as house cleaning, lawn maintenance, and fuel oil delivery. They can also include people such as the music teachers, child-care providers, and medical service providers who come to your home routinely.

Home services should be canceled ahead of time as a courtesy to the provider, and so you do not incur unexpected cancellation penalties. Refer to the checklist in Appendix A for a comprehensive list of services to cancel before you move and to restart after you move.

Request a Gypsy Moth Inspection Form

If you are moving outdoor plants or regulated outdoor household articles and traveling from an area infested with the gypsy moth (most of the states in the Northeast) to one that is not infested, request a gypsy moth inspection form. Inquire in advance about this inspection with your moving company, or check the Internet for requirements in your state, or contact the U.S. Department of Agriculture for more information. Gypsy moth caterpillars can devastate hardwood forests, so it's important to prevent their spread.

After the inspection has been completed, the signed form must accompany your household shipment. Without it, your possessions may be detained if the truck is stopped for inspection en route. The inspection form documents that any outdoor articles in your shipment are free of gypsy moths and their larva. This inspection is required by law in some states, and failure to comply may result in penalties.

CHAPTER SEVEN

Packing Days

The first time my family moved, my husband and I packed all of the boxes ourselves. I had to go to the grocery store at six o'clock every morning before work to retrieve boxes before they were broken down. I also brought home empty copy paper boxes from work every day. It was a huge undertaking. I didn't have any packing advice, and many of the items I packed were broken or crushed when I unpacked them. Since I had packed the boxes myself, I was not eligible to file a claim with the moving company. I was devastated!

If you are not hiring moving help, this chapter is going to assist you enormously. You will learn where to get packing supplies at reasonable prices, how to pack your belongings so that they do not get damaged, how to properly mark your boxes, and how to properly disconnect, move, and reconnect large appliances and high-tech equipment.

Even if your move is a corporate relocation, you'll find many tips in this chapter to make your move go smoother than you ever imagined! There are tips for moving pets and plants, packing a survival box, and eliminating hazardous materials. In addition, you'll learn how to move and protect high-value items.

If you are packing yourself, begin by packing all items seldom used. If a moving company will do your packing, begin by organizing your belongings so that they get packed logically.

Gather Boxes and Packing Supplies

A good source for boxes is the local grocery store, liquor store, or drugstore. Ask the store manager in advance for boxes. Small stores may receive shipments only once a week and will give away boxes only if you are there at a specified time to pick them up. For instance, some stores unpack boxes at 6:00 A.M. and break down and dispose of them immediately. Only the early bird will get these containers! Collect both large and small boxes. If you know people who have recently moved, they may be willing to donate their unwanted boxes to you.

Photocopier paper boxes are strong and have tight-fitting lids. Large offices and print shops have an ample supply daily. If you don't have access to these boxes, check with friends, relatives, or neighbors.

New boxes can be purchased at many moving companies, at self-storage and trailer-rental locations, and at packaging stores. Previously used boxes are sometimes available free of charge or for a nominal fee from the moving company.

Wardrobe boxes are an excellent way to move clothing, tall lamps, and awkward items. Mattress boxes are also available. They may be purchased from the moving company or at many self-storage and trailer-rental locations.

For delicate items, you may want to purchase special packing boxes (dish-pack boxes) to ensure safe moving and ink-free materials to avoid the possibility of ink rubbing off on your possessions. Unprinted newspaper stock (also referred to as newsprint or packing paper) and tissue paper are available from moving companies, packaging stores, and large office supply stores.

In fact, you will need plenty of packing supplies. Newspapers are an excellent, inexpensive packing material for nondelicate items. If you do not have enough newspapers, neighbors are usually willing to donate their copies to the cause.

Finally, have lots of black markers and packing tape on hand. Label your boxes, and tape them generously. You don't want the bottom of your boxes to fall apart during transit. Make sure all boxes are clearly marked with a general description of their contents and the name of the room to which they should be delivered at your new location. For boxes containing breakable items, mark them as follows with a thick black marker: "FRAGILE—TOP—DO NOT TURN UPSIDE DOWN."

Precious items at high risk of damage are best moved by hand when possible. You will want to make a written note of where you packed unusual items to save time locating them when you unpack. If you are only moving a short distance, wrap mattresses and furniture in old sheets or blankets to protect them from gathering dirt or developing scratches, pack glass items in dishcloths, and wrap small pictures or mirrors in towels. If you are moving yourself, you can rent a dolly on moving day from a rental store to move large boxes, refrigerators, washers and dryers, etc.

Items Going to a Temporary Storage Facility

If you need to place furniture, boxes, or appliances in temporary storage, remember to make a complete list of each item going to storage and the exact contents of each box. Clean rugs, draperies, wall hangings, refrigerators, and freezers before sending them to storage so that they don't develop mildew and deteriorate while in storage.

Only store items that you *will not* need, since sometimes things remain in storage longer than intended. For instance, do not put children's shoes or clothing in storage unless they have already outgrown them. If the clothes were to remain in storage for one year instead of three months, then the clothing may no longer fit. You would have lost out.

Once your boxes are in storage, retrieving them can be expensive. Call at least three weeks in advance to retrieve items from a temporary storage facility.

The storage of motor vehicles and boats is not usually covered under a corporate relocation agreement. You will have to make your own arrangements for storing such items.

Items Requiring Special Handling

If you still have the original cartons for the following items, use the boxes to repackage your items. Before disconnecting and packing electronic components, draw a diagram or take a photo of how the wiring is connected to save yourself time when reconnecting the components at your destination. Movers will not reconnect your stereo system, VCR, DVD player, video games, answering machine, or computer equipment.

Videocassette Recorders and DVD Players

Remove tapes and disks and close doors before packing. (Be careful not to push the door open with paper). Pack the box flat, not on its side. After packing, label the box "VCR [or DVD player]—FRAGILE—TOP—DO NOT TURN ON SIDE OR UPSIDE DOWN."

Compact Disc Players

Remove CDs from the player before packing. Then lock the CD unit. (Most players have a lock underneath the unit.) Locking the player will prevent damage caused by vibration in transit. After packing, label the box "CD PLAYER—FRAGILE—TOP—DO NOT TURN ON SIDE OR UPSIDE DOWN."

Stereo Turntable

Remove records from the player before packing. Lock the turntable using the lock-down on the underside of the plate or on the inside near the tone arm. Put protective guards on the cartridge and stylus. The cartridge should be removed or properly secured before the turntable is packed. After packing, label the box "STEREO TURNTABLE—FRAGILE—TOP—DO NOT TURN ON SIDE OR UPSIDE DOWN."

Big-Screen Televisions

Pack the TV in the original box, if available, or wrap the unit in a moving pad and tape the pad together. (Especially protect the front of the screen.) After packing, label the box "TV—FRAGILE—TOP—DO NOT TURN ON SIDE OR UPSIDE DOWN."

Computers and Printers

Computers (monitor, CPU, and keyboard) and printers are especially susceptible to damage during transit. Follow these simple steps to protect your computer from mechanical failure or damage due to normal physical shock that can occur during transport:

1. Back up all data from your hard drive onto a tape or other backup device.

2. Remove diskettes from the drives and close the drive doors.

3. Turn off the power supply. Then remove all cables from the back of the units.

4. For the computer, use the original packing containers if possible; the rigid Styrofoam inserts will hold the system securely in place. If you do not have the original packing materials, use a sturdy packing box and pack firmly to prevent movement during transit. After packing, label the boxes "COMPUTER (MONITOR, CPU, KEYBOARD)—FRAGILE—TOP—DO NOT TURN ON SIDE OR UPSIDE DOWN."

5. For the printer, use the original packing container and Styrofoam forms for both ink-jet and laser printers. If the original packing is not available, use a sturdy box slightly larger than the printer and pack firmly. When moving a laser printer, remove the toner cartridge so that the powdered ink will not spill during transit and contaminate the engine. After packing, label the box "PRINTER—FRAGILE—TOP—DO NOT TURN ON SIDE OR UPSIDE DOWN."

Glass-Top and Marble-Top Tables, Oversize Mirrors, and Artwork

A specialty services company can be hired to crate all large glass-top and marble-top tables, oversize mirrors, and collections of artwork to prevent damage to these fragile objects. A designated person will be sent to your house to crate and then to uncrate these pieces.

Pianos

If you are moving locally, contact a piano mover to move your piano. Reputable moving companies will always take extra care when moving your upright or baby grand. *Do not* have your friends try to move a piano unless you rent a piano dolly. Not using the right dolly may cause more damage to them, or to the piano, than it is worth.

Grandfather and Grandmother Clocks

Remove chimes, weights, and pendulums. Wrap these components in tissue paper, and then wrap again in packing paper or place in a small box. Label and tape package accordingly. Then tie or tape the clock door closed so that it does not open during transit. If taping, use removable tape so you do not destroy the finish on the clock.

Pool Tables, Ping-Pong Tables, Arcade Games, etc.

Disassemble these objects when possible and wrap in moving pads to prevent scratches.

Sewing Machines

Do not leave the machine in the sewing table. Take the machine out and pack it separately. If a sewing machine is moved in a sewing machine table and the table is turned upside down when it is loaded in the truck, vibrations occurring during transit can cause machine parts to break.

Water Beds

Empty the water out of your mattress. Moving companies will not empty the mattress for you. Hire a specialty services company to perform this job if you choose not to do it yourself. The moving company will usually disassemble and then reassemble the bed frame, but it is a good idea to inquire about this service ahead of time.

Tough-to-Pack Items

Outdoor play sets, canoes, surfboards, skis, bicycles. It's difficult to put these in a box. It's best to tie or tape them to minimize abrasions, or to wrap them in a moving pad for protection.

Aquariums and hot tubs. Disconnect, drain the water, clean out, and wrap appropriately in a moving pad for protection.

Satellite dish. Put it in the original box, or wrap it in a moving pad for protection.

Photo Albums and Photos

Organize your photos if you have not done so already. To do this, gather all of your photos into one place. Separate the negatives from the printed pictures. Buy photo boxes and store your photos in chronological order, then label the outside of each box by subject and date. Buy archival photo negative pages from your photo store, and organize negatives by subject and date. The moving company will move your photos, but it is best to pack negatives with other important documents. That way if there is an accident on the truck or your box of photos is lost in transit, you will be able to get reprints made of your missing photos. If you have scrapbooking photo albums, pack them in a box within a box, or hand carry a few of these albums with you. You will have peace of mind knowing that they are in your safekeeping.

Ready-to-Assemble, Particleboard, and Veneer Furnishings

Many moving companies will not move preassembled particle board furniture, such as big entertainment centers, computer work stations, bookcases, and garage utility cabinets.

Particleboard furniture does not travel well: The veneer chips and flakes, especially along the bottom edges; the dowels or nails fall out and are lost; and the glue loosens. Since there is no easy fix for these problems, many moving companies will no longer move particleboard furniture. If the moving company does agree to move the furniture for you, it will be moved at your own risk. (*Note:* Any damage to such items incurred during transit will *not* be covered by your moving company.)

Fragile Items

Dishes. Pack in a type of packing box known as a dish-pack box. Crumple up packing paper and put it in the bottom of the box. Wrap each dish in packing paper, on the diagonal, using two sheets at a time. Nest four to five plates together in the double sheets of paper, then fold and wrap together. (For very delicate dishes, wrap in tissue paper before using the packing paper.) Place the wrapped package in the box, plates standing on their edges—*never lay plates flat.* Place the heaviest dishes on the bottom of the box and the lighter dishes on top. Label the box "DISHES—FRAGILE—TOP—DO NOT TURN ON SIDE OR UPSIDE DOWN."

Bowls. Pack and label the same as for dishes, except nest only up to three bowls at a time and turn the bowls upside down in the box.

Expensive stemware. Carefully stuff tissue paper inside each glass. Then wrap the outside with tissue paper. Next, wrap each glass in packing paper on the diagonal. Cut a piece of corrugated cardboard slightly longer than the stemware, wrap around the packing paper and tape together. Then place it in a dish-pack box upside down. Never pack stemware on its side.

Knives. Wrap in several pieces of packing paper and tape together. Mark the outside of the package "KNIVES" to prevent injury during unpacking. Place in a packing box.

Lamps. Unplug and remove the shade, lightbulb, and fittings. Wind the cord. Place the lamp on its side and wrap in tissue paper. Then wrap it diagonally in packing paper. Wrap the bulb and fittings separately, tape, and label. Place the lamp, bulb, and fittings in a box with crumpled packing paper on the bottom. Place the shade in a separate box surrounded by packing paper. Pack only one shade per box to prevent denting or cracking.

Large Appliances

On moving day, follow these instructions to move stoves, washing machines and dryers, air conditioners, refrigerators and freezers, microwave ovens, electric heaters, etc.

1. Disconnect the appliance from its power source.

2. Remove parts that can fall off or cause damage. Pack these parts in a separate box and label appropriately.

3. Turn off faucets and disconnect any drain hoses.

4. Tape the electrical cord to the back of the appliance, and then tape the door shut. (Use removable tape that will not destroy the finish on the appliance.)

5. Before moving day, remember to clean and dry the inside of refrigerators and freezers. Leave the doors ajar so the appliance can air out and dry thoroughly. Drain the icemaker hose.

6. Wrap the appliance in a moving pad, or pack it in a large box to keep it from getting scratched. Label the box appropriately. If you are moving the appliance yourself, rent a moving dolly.

Animals

Quite simply, animals *cannot* be shipped in moving vans under any circumstances. Moving animals will be your own responsibility. Contact your veterinarian or local pet store for specific guidelines on how to transport your pets properly. These are general guidelines:

If moving a horse, rent a horse trailer. Dogs and cats can sometimes ride in the car passenger seat, or for safety they may be caged or crated. They will need to be placed in a cage or a crate if you take them on an airplane. Contact the airline for detailed instructions when taking an animal on an airplane. Make sure your pet is wearing its collar and tags in case it gets lost.

If you are going a short distance, fish can be put in a plastic bag. Check with your local aquarium store for tips on transporting fish long-distance. Don't forget to drain and clean your fish tank.

Most small pets such as mice, hamsters, and birds travel best in their own cages. Make sure they have plenty of food and water. Keep small pets out of drafts and extreme temperatures, and cover their cages to keep them calm during transit.

Plants

Check with the U.S. Department of Agriculture for federal and state regulations about transporting of houseplants by a commercial carrier. Some movers will discourage you from moving your indoor plants because plants are not guaranteed under any circumstance. Movers will also warn you about plants going into shock and never fully recovering. That said, I have had many truck drivers who will gladly move plants. They consider the plants to be part of the family.

The truth is, plants can be moved, but only at certain times of year. Houseplants *cannot* survive the frost of winter or the extreme heat of summer in the back of a moving van on a long-distance move. However, under temperate conditions, plants can usually be moved without dying. They may go into shock, but the damage should be short-lived (approximately one to three months) if you care for the plants properly on arrival at your new destination.

Plants have a good chance of surviving a move if you follow these four guidelines:

1. Wrap small plants in packing paper, leaving an opening above each plant, and place the plants in a box. Cut holes in the sides of the box to provide air. Tie large plants—whether packed in a box or placed in the moving van—with string to keep them from moving around or breaking during transit. Hanging plants can be hung on a metal rack in a wardrobe carton.

Tie the handle of the plant hanger to the rack to prevent it from falling off during transit.

2. Water your plants thoroughly the day before they are loaded onto the truck—except if the temperature is below freezing, in which case water them lightly to prevent the roots from freezing during transit. Most houseplants can survive up to ten days without additional watering.

3. Load your plants on the truck last so that they come off the truck first at your destination. Most houseplants can tolerate darkness for up to a week.

4. Water your plants as soon as they are unloaded. (Most drivers will unload your plants the day they arrive at your new destination, even if the truck is not scheduled to be unloaded until the following day.) Remove dead leaves or damaged limbs, and give them plenty of water and fertilizer. You will be pleasantly surprised at how quickly they recover.

Great Self-Packing Techniques

1. Get your supplies ready: boxes, packing paper, bubble wrap, wide packing tape, removable tape, scissors, box cutters, black felt-tip markers, resealable plastic bags, and toolbox.

2. Pack one room at a time.

3. Limit each carton to a weight of less than thirty pounds. No huge boxes, please!

4. Place heavier items on the bottom of a carton, and place similar items together in one carton.

5. Put light items in larger boxes and heavy items (such as books and record albums) in smaller boxes.

6. Pack delicate items together. Do not pack delicate items with heavy items (such as glassware with heavy pots).

7. Wrap objects carefully with newspaper, packing paper, or tissue paper. You can also use towels and sheets as packing materials. Make sure all objects are securely positioned in the box so that they will not move during transit.

8. Pack your kitchen last so that you may use it as long as possible. Dish-pack cartons can be purchased to protect your dishes, plates, and glassware. Extra-sturdy cardboard boxes can be substituted for dish-pack cartons.

9. When packing glass picture frames, wrap them in newspaper or packing paper to prevent the glass and frames from rubbing against the box. Before placing the frames in a shipping box, line the bottom and sides of each box with crumpled packing paper for extra cushioning. Then place each frame in a special picture frame box or strong cardboard box and add more crumpled paper to the top of the box before taping it shut. If the frames are small, place several frames together in a medium-size box then put packing paper between each frame and on the top and bottom of each box to prevent movement during transit.

10. Keep small parts such as screws and knobs with the object to which they belong by placing them in a resealable plastic bag and taping them securely to the back of the furniture or inside a drawer. Do not pack tools needed to reassemble furniture. Keep those tools with you to expedite reassembly at your new location.

11. Take picture hooks out of the walls, and place in a resealable plastic bag.

12. Tape appliance, stereo equipment, television, and computer operating instructions to the item, or put the instructions aside for safekeeping in a "survival box." (See the next section for details about survival boxes.)

13. Put the remote controls to your television set and stereo equipment in your survival box.

14. Dresser drawers may be packed with lightweight clothing, but remove liquids, breakables, or valuable items. Contain medicines, perfumes, lotions, nail polish, and other liquids in resealable plastic bags. Then wrap the bags in bubble wrap and place in a box. Remove adjustable shelves from cabinets, bookshelves, or dressers before moving.

15. Candles, CDs, DVDs, records, tapes, undeveloped film, and floppy disks are susceptible to heat damage if they travel long-distance in a moving van during hot weather. To prevent damage, carry these items with you or ship them yourself via an express service to reduce transit time.

16. Disassemble floor lamps when possible, and pack them in a box or wrap with a moving pad. Tape the moving pad to hold it in place.

17. Pack each lamp shade individually in a box surrounded by packing paper to prevent the shade from getting bent or smashed.

18. Take lightbulbs out of lamps and pack them carefully to prevent breakage.

19. Number your boxes in sequential order with numbered stickers and label them on the top and sides, in the same position on each box, with a thick

felt-tip marker. For boxes with delicate items, label the box "FRAGILE—TOP LOAD ONLY." List your name, the room in which the items belong, and the box's contents as shown:

> Last Name
> Meghan's Bedroom
> Contents: shoes, books, dolls, stuffed animals, pillows

20. Schedule enough time to pack all of your boxes. For a family of four, plan on taking at least one full day to pack each room in the house, with the kitchen, office, basement and garage taking two to three days each. Remember to schedule time to pack the bathrooms, hall closets, and pictures hanging on the walls. You don't want to be caught off guard with unpacked items on moving day. You will get the packing accomplished more quickly if you have someone helping you. Estimate your time carefully.

Survival Box

Pack a box of items that you will need immediately after your move. Mark it "SURVIVAL BOX—OPEN IMMEDIATELY—PLACE ON KITCHEN COUNTER." Load this box on the truck last so it will come off the truck first. Start collecting the items for this box early so that it can be partially packed the final week before your move. Leave room in the box to add last-minute items on moving day. It should contain such things as:

- Paper plates, cups, and napkins
- Eating utensils
- Pots and pans
- Canned or boxed food items
- Snacks
- Coffee machine, coffee mugs, coffee, filters, and sugar packets
- Remote controls to the television and stereo equipment (remove batteries if the move is long-distance)
- Instruction manuals
- Kids' toys (remove any batteries), videos, etc.
- Baby supplies

■ Telephone, answering machine, and telephone list

■ Paper towels, tissues, and toilet paper

■ Soap

■ Cleaning supplies

■ Alarm clock/radio (remove any batteries)

■ Dishcloth and towels

■ Can opener/wine opener

■ Wine/champagne glasses

■ Keys to clocks, cabinets, jewelry chest, etc.

■ Household lightbulbs and a flashlight (remove batteries)

■ First-aid kit: aspirin, tweezers, bandages, antiseptics, prescriptions, etc.

■ Pet food and supplies

■ Toolbox supplies and picture hooks that you have removed from your walls

Also include any items that will make the first few days in your new location go more smoothly. You may also want to mark your stereo equipment, television, and computer boxes and linen boxes (blankets, sheets, towels, and shower curtain) with the words "OPEN IMMEDIATELY." Hand carry removed batteries with you. The goal of preparing a survival box is to get your life back to normal as quickly as possible after your move.

Martha's Moving Survival Tips

The remote control just walked away! We sold our big-screen television to the new owners of the house. However, the packers inadvertently packed the remote control. I discovered the remote when I was unpacking at the new house, and I immediately mailed the remote to the new owners with an apologetic note for the inconvenience. Courtesy counts in a move and is always greatly appreciated.

Box of Cleaning Supplies

If you do not plan to hire a cleaning service to clean your house after it is empty, you will need to pack a box of cleaning supplies to do this job yourself (refer to the checklist in Chapter Eight). Pack this box the final week prior to your move. Since the movers cannot transport cleaning supplies in the moving van (refer to the section of this chapter called Eliminating Hazardous Materials), after you have finished cleaning your house you will need to move this box in your own car, dispose of the supplies appropriately, or donate them to a neighbor or to cleaning personnel. Add the names of supplies that you dispose of to the list of items to replace after the move. You'll find this list in Appendix B.

Box of Items for the New Owners

If you sell your home, remember to leave a box of appropriate items for the new owners. Mark the box "TO THE NEW OWNERS—DO NOT LOAD ON TRUCK." This box should contain product warranty instruction manuals and a list of service providers, with names and phone numbers:

___ Stove (cooktop) manual	___ Sprinkler system manual
___ Oven manual	___ Garage door opener(s)
___ Microwave manual	___ Television/remote control
___ Dishwasher manual	___ Jacuzzi manual
___ Refrigerator manual	___ Pool or spa manual
___ Garbage disposal manual	___ Fountain manual
___ Water softener manual	___ Homeowner's manual
___ Hot-water heater manual	___ Local telephone books
___ Furnace manual	___ Neighborhood telephone directory
___ Humidifier manual	___ Local maps
___ Swamp cooler manual	___ House blueprints or floor plans
___ Central vacuum system manual	___ Lawn service provider
___ Gas fireplace manual	___ Builder's name and phone number
___ Thermostat manual	___ Pool service provider
___ Security system manual	___ Snow removal service provider

Eliminating Hazardous Materials

Moving companies cannot transport potentially hazardous items. Most moving companies have identified the following household items as potentially hazardous. This list includes typical household cleaning products that can produce deadly gases or could spontaneously combust when mixed with other chemicals. By knowing about this list ahead of time, you can save time and money by using up these products. Or you might prefer to dispose of them appropriately before moving day. Your community may have a day where household hazardous material and unwanted appliances can be dropped off free of charge or for a small fee. Check your community newsletter or municipal Web site for postings. Alternatively, if you are moving locally, you can transport hazardous items in your own vehicle.

Common Household Products

- Batteries
- Cans or bottles of soda and beer
- Champagne and opened bottles of wine or alcohol
- Vinegar

Common Household Cleaning Products

- Ammonia and bleach
- Dishwashing liquid
- Laundry detergent

Combustible Liquids

- Antifreeze compounds
- Camphor oil
- Disinfectants
- Type cleaners (fluids containing combustible material, e.g., spot for clothing, liquid cleaners for office machines)

Corrosive Liquids

- Acids (such as photographic chemicals used in developing film)
- Etching acid
- Iron/steel rust-preventing compounds
- Sulphuric and muriatic acid

Explosives

- Small arms ammunition (This is not completely prohibited from shipment, but it is prohibited from shipment by a household goods or an unaccompanied baggage carrier.)
- Black powder
- Brick matches
- Brick noisemakers (firecrackers)
- Cigarette loads
- Dynamite, plastic, or similar explosives
- Explosive auto alarms
- Explosive flashbulbs
- Fireworks
- Loaded weapons
- Primers
- Smokeless powder
- Souvenir explosives
- Spearguns with charged heads

Flammables

- Adhesives (glue, cements, plastics)
- Aerosol cans (flammables include hair spray, deodorants, perfumes, colognes)
- Charcoal briquettes
- Cleaning fluids
- Compound three-weed killers
- Enamel
- Gasoline (Gasoline must be removed from lawn mower, trimmer, and any other gas-powered device before shipment.)
- Hand-signal flares
- Kerosene
- Lacquer
- Leather dressing

- Lighter fluids (pocket, charcoal camp stove, lamp, or torch)
- Matches
- Nail polish and nail polish remover
- Oil stains for wood
- Paint and varnish remover
- Paint (flammable)
- Petroleum products (kerosene, gas, oil)
- Photographic flashbulbs and lamps
- Polishes (liquid, metal, stove, wood)
- Propane or other gas used for cooking or heating purposes
- Propane tanks (non-purged)
- Rags soaked in flammable or corrosive substances
- Shellac, stains, and varnish
- Shoe polish (liquid)
- Solvents (plastic)
- Turpentine
- Windshield solvent
- Wines
- Wood filler

Gases (Compressed)

- Engine-starting fluids
- Fire extinguishers
- Gases used in welding
- Scuba-diving tanks (unless completely empty)

Eliminating Items Not Authorized for Shipment

In many corporate relocations the following items will not be authorized for shipment, although some may be negotiable under your corporate relocation agreement if discussed in advance. If you choose to move these items, you will need to get your own estimate from a moving company and pay for the cost out of your own pocket.

- Construction materials (such as fireplace wood, flagstone, bricks, stone, and lumber)

- Live plants, shrubs, and trees (If the moving company has authorized moving your plants, refer to the tips earlier in this chapter to help your plants survive during transit.)

- All perishable food goods and open liquor containers

- Animals (household pets, fish, horses, cattle, fowl, etc.)

- Large supplies of food, grain, mulch, or water

- Tractors and farm and heavy equipment (not including lawn and garden equipment)

- Watercraft or trailers exceeding 30 feet (or shorter in length if the craft or trailer will not fit in the van)

- Items of unusual weight or bulk (such as a large, heavy rock collection)

- Motor homes, campers, and trailers

Protecting High-Value Items and Valuable Documents

To guard against theft or loss, it is advisable *not* to load the following types of high-value items on a moving van, especially if your inventory will be placed in a storage facility for any length of time. Many of these items have a high resale value in the black market and are small enough to unknowingly slip into the wrong hands. Your valuable documents could even pose a threat to your identity if stolen. If at all possible, hand-carry these items to their final destination. Alternatively, you can ship them by certified mail or UPS, but keep the receipt in your purse or briefcase for safekeeping.

If you do decide to place high-value items in the moving van, make sure that the appraisal documents are in your possession (and not loaded onto the moving van) and that the items are accurately documented on the high-value items list. Review this list with the driver before you sign it and the final bill of lading.

High-value items include:

- Cash and coin collections
- Rare documents
- Stamp collections
- Irreplaceable collector's memorabilia
- Precious stones (not in settings)
- Valuable jewelry (not costume jewelry)
- Valuable documents: your will or living trust; insurance policies; birth, marriage, and death certificates; religious certificates; appraisal documents; and securities (stock certificates, bonds, etc.)

Protecting High-Value Inventory

High-value inventory is different from high-value items because it includes objects that are bulky, are often heavy, and may require crating services or special packing techniques to ensure their safety. High-value inventory will need to be transported in the moving van. However, it must be properly identified and documented before it is loaded. Your moving coordinator will help you to identify high-value inventory when you complete your initial moving estimate.

High-value inventory includes any item in excess of $100 per pound per article. These high-value objects must be properly identified on the mover's high-value inventory checklist. You will need to fill in a description and the appraised value of the inventory on this checklist. If these objects have not been recently appraised, have them appraised before you move to make sure that the amount you put down is substantiated. If any of these objects are damaged or loss in transit, you must provide a copy of the appraisal documents to the moving company to justify your claim. A photo of the item would also assist with the settlement of the claim.

High-value inventory may include:

- Antiques
- China sets
- Museum-quality pieces
- Crystal
- Figurines
- Furs and fur coats
- Fine art
- Oriental rugs
- Rare books
- Silverware
- Silver service sets

CHAPTER EIGHT

The Final Week

I enjoy the final week in the moving process. This is when the move starts to feel like it's really going to happen. I begin to remove pictures from the walls, order take-out food more often, and start packing my travel suitcase. These days, I am fortunate enough to have moving personnel arrive at my house to start packing my belongings. A whirlwind of organized activity puts the excitement of moving into the air. My husband is usually out of town on business during this week, and I can now rely on my teenage children to help out with the move. They have the final week checklist practically memorized after all of our moves.

It is also a bittersweet time when I realize that there is no turning back. Neighbors drop by to say good-bye, and my house begins to feel less and less like my home. This is when I focus on the excitement of my new life that lies ahead.

If you have been following the steps in this moving guide, the final week should go smoothly and be quite manageable.

Seven Days to Go

■ Call utility companies and request transfer and turn on or turn off of service. (Refer to the utilities worksheets in Appendix B.) Provide with disconnecting/connecting dates and a forwarding address and phone number. The utility company will need forwarding information to refund your deposit and to send you a final bill. Note that some companies require an advance cash deposit in person (or by mail) before they will provide service to you.

■ Dispose of all perishable food supplies you will not consume before moving day.

■ Call your lender to verify that your loan has received final authorization.

■ Review and continue to complete items on the Comprehensive Moving Checklist in Appendix A.

■ _____

■ _____

■ _____

■ _____

Six Days to Go

■ Make any special transportation arrangements for a disabled person, an elderly person, or a pregnant woman who is experiencing medical complications.

■ Arrange babysitting for moving day.

■ Arrange for the transport of pets.

■ Take pets to the veterinarian for immunizations.

■ Clean out wood-burning fireplaces and charcoal barbecue grills. Remove partially burned logs, coals, soot, and ashes. Then brush or vacuum clean.

■ Submit a change-of-address form to your local post office, or complete this step online at www.monstermoving.com.

■ Continue packing your survival box. If you are using hired packers, gather items to be placed in this box before the packers arrive. (Refer to the checklist in Chapter Seven.)

■ _____

■ _____

■ _____

■ _____

Five Days to Go

■ Take down draperies and curtains only if they are specifically excluded from the sale of your house and this exclusion is documented in writing in your real estate contract. (In most cases you will want to leave the rods on the windows because they usually will not fit windows in your new residence.) Check your real estate contract, and talk to your real estate agent before removing any drapery rods or draperies. Note that moving personnel are not authorized to take down draperies or rods or any other object that is screwed or nailed into a door or wall.

■ Take down fixtures screwed or nailed into walls or doors that have been designated in your real estate contract as exclusions from the sale of your home.

■ Wash, dry-clean, or air out draperies before having them packed.

■ Complete packing the box of items for the new owners. (Refer to the checklist in Chapter Seven.)

■ Tell the movers when you want the unpackers to arrive at your new residence.

■ _____

■ _____

■ _____

■ _____

Four Days to Go

■ Dust frames and clean glass on all picture frames and artwork.

■ Call your real estate agents and moving coordinator to make sure your move is on schedule.

■ Return library books.

■ Pick up photos from the photo store.

■ Pick up prescription medicine from the drugstore.

■ Pick up items in storage.

■ Pick up clothes from the cleaners. (Recycle extra metal hangers by returning them to the cleaners.)

- Print out driving direction to your new address for the driver. Use your computer to print out accurate directions, mileage information, and a map to your new location. Internet sites such as www.yahoo .com (go to Maps) can quickly provide this type of information.

- _____

- _____

- _____

- _____

Three Days to Go

- Clean the refrigerator and the freezer (defrost if necessary). Dispose of opened containers of food that you will not consume by moving day.

- Drain the grease out of your electric fryer. Clean and prepare for packing.

- Empty the water out of your cappuccino or coffee maker and clean thoroughly.

- If you are moving to a high-rise building, reserve the freight elevator.

- Empty and close your safe-deposit box.

- Empty and close your post office box.

- Cut the grass, if applicable. Then dispose of any gasoline remaining in the lawn mower or gas can appropriately.

- If you are moving to a gated community with a staffed gate, inform the management of your move-in date so that the moving van will be allowed access through the gate.

- _____

- _____

- _____

- _____

Two Days to Go

- Pack a box of cleaning supplies if you do not plan to hire a cleaning service. Mark this box "CLEANING SUPPLIES—DO NOT LOAD ON TRUCK." The relocation company, or your real estate agent, may deduct funds from your account for a poorly cleaned house. Refer to Chapter Seven for a list of cleaning products that cannot be transported in the moving van.

Bucket	Broom, dustpan, and brush
Mop	Kitchen cleaning products
Floor cleaner	Bathroom cleaning products
Sponges or rags	Toilet cleaner and brush
Towels	Glass cleaner
Paper towels	Vacuum cleaner

_____	_____
_____	_____
_____	_____

■ Clean the inside and outside of your appliances: oven, stove, microwave, and dishwasher (unless a cleaning service will do this job).

■ Deplete, or properly dispose of, the gas tank to your gas barbecue grill and camping stove.

■ Dust furniture, but do not wax or polish. (Furniture pads may stick to the waxed or polished finish during hot weather and damage your furniture. Polished furniture is also very slippery to pick up.)

■ Clean the bathrooms (unless a cleaning service will do this job).

■ Return video rentals to the video store.

■ Provide information to authorize the wire transfer of house closing funds.

■ Call lender to verify that your loan is scheduled to fund on time.

■ Schedule the final walk-through on the new house, preferably held the day before the house closing date.

One Day to Go

■ Pack a suitcase or box full of travel gear. Tell the movers not to load this suitcase/box on the truck. Label with a sign that reads "DO NOT LOAD ON TRUCK."

Clothing and jewelry	Sunglasses, eyeglasses, and contact
Personal grooming supplies	lenses
Batteries	Medicine and prescriptions
Portable safe with family	Camera, film, and/or video camera
medical and school records	Real estate documents
Moving documents	Checkbook
Cellular phone or pager	Keys and directions to your
Purse or wallet	new house
	Medical identification cards

■ If driving long-distance to your destination, also include the following items in your suitcase or box:

Maps and driving directions	Address Book
Children's toys and necessities	Snacks and drinks
Videos (if auto has a VCR)	Coins (for tolls along the way)
Emergency supplies	Pet Supplies (cages, ID tags, leash, food, water)

■ Sweep, power blow, or hose down (or shovel when required) the walkways and driveway so the movers do not track dirt (or snow) into your house.

■ Completely empty the refrigerator and freezer of food.

■ Wash your towels, sheets, and bedding so they will be clean and ready to use the first or second night at your new location.

■ Clean out animal litter boxes (or cages) and food bowls. Drain the fish tank.

■ Be ready with the correct payment method (cash, money order, or certified check) to pay the driver on moving day. Most moving companies do not take credit cards or personal checks.

■ _____

■ _____

Transporting Your Motor Vehicle

If your motor vehicle is going to be transported in the moving van or on a car-carrier truck, reduce the gas level to *one-fourth* of a tank and check the antifreeze and oil to make sure these levels are at *full* prior to loading day. Empty every item out of your vehicle, including insurance and motor vehicle documents, and put those documents with your transport documents. Make sure that the transporter personnel documents all scratches and dents before the car is loaded. (If you wash your car before ship-ment, such surface details will be easier to identify and will eliminate arguments over discrepancies at your final destination.) Verify that the correct mileage and license plate number is recorded on the transport document. You and the transporter per-sonnel must sign this document. This is the contract between you and the moving company and your only receipt for your vehicle. You'll need to present this receipt to transporter personnel to retrieve your vehicle at its final destination.

Make sure the driver has a contact name and number and the delivery address (your new house or work facility). Ask the driver or your moving coordinator for the expected delivery dates. Make sure someone will be available to receive the vehicle at its final destination. Automobiles are not usually authorized for storage under your corporate relocation agreement.

Even if your vehicle will be transported in the moving van, do not pack any boxes or miscellaneous items in your vehicle. Damage could occur because those items will not be securely tied down during transit. In addition, the insurance com-pany will not cover any items left in your vehicle in the event of damage, theft, or an accident.

If your move is a corporate relocation, you may be charged extra to transport more than one vehicle or a recreational vehicle. Check your relocation agreement for details.

The Packers Have Arrived

It you have an exemplary packing crew at your house for three or four days, you can have fun during this part of the move. At last, someone else is doing some of the work for you, and if you are lucky, you might get a crew with a good sense of humor. I had such luck on my last move. Two dedicated packers (who were also in charge of loading the truck) made this move the best ever. After reading the preliminary copy of *The Moving Survival Guide* one night, they brought me a box labeled "survival breakfast kit" from the local bakery the next morning. The box was full of treats: muffins, doughnuts, and bagels. We laughed about it all day! They were hard workers who really enjoyed their job, and they helped to make that move unforgettable.

If you're fortunate enough to have professional packers, let them do the pack-ing. Anything that is *not* packed by them *will not* be covered by the moving company if damaged. They are experts at packing and know how to pack to minimize dam-age during transport.

1. Confirm the date and time the truck will be loaded with the moving company. Packing can take from one to three days, depending on the quantity of your belongings and the number of packers sent to your house.

2. Be present to supervise during packing. The packers will have many questions and will need your assistance to do a good job. Designate the identification names you want written on the boxes (For example: Brian's Room, Living Room, Office, Playroom, etc.). Tape these names to a door or wall.

3. Packers are fast and efficient. (They are like the ocean; you never want to turn your back on them. Their job is to pack everything in sight!)

4. Make sure the dishwasher is empty or full of *clean* dishes. (I have had inexperienced packers pack dirty dishes left in the dishwasher.)

5. Make sure the washer and dryer are empty. (Inexperienced packers have been known to pack dirty and wet clothes from the washer when they packed the laundry room.)

6. Make sure the packers do not box up the oven or microwave racks. If these racks are currently stored in a drawer, put them in the oven and/or microwave to prevent the packers from accidentally packing them.

7. Remove any bedding remaining on beds. (Packers will not do this for you.)

8. The packers will remove pictures from the walls, but they will not remove the picture hooks. Remove the hooks yourself, and place them in a resealable plastic bag or tape them securely to the backs of pictures.

9. If the refrigerator is being moved, empty it, unplug it, and leave the door ajar. (Packers will not empty and clean your refrigerator for you.) If you have an ice maker hooked up, unplug it from the back of the refrigerator and drain all water from the tube. (When moving during freezing weather, be extra careful to completely drain this tube the day before moving to prevent freezing and cracking of the tube during transit.)

Martha's Moving Survival Tips

It's 8:00 A.M.! Where are the packers? Call your moving coordinator or the moving company immediately and find out why the packers have not shown up at your house at the scheduled time. If you are paying for the job by the hour, make sure you are not charged for time until the packers officially commence packing.

10. Remove all batteries from clocks, radios, flashlights, etc. Put batteries in a resealable plastic bag, and place with those personal belongings that will not be loaded onto the truck. (The movers cannot transport batteries in the moving van on long-distance moves.)

11. Finish any final personal packing. Also pack all of the shoes that the family will need in one box. Label this box, "FAMILY SHOES—LOAD LAST." When you get to your new house, you will be able to find your shoes quickly so that you can get dressed for work, go out to dinner, or locate your favorite slippers.

12. If you are packing open food boxes and bags (such as flour, sugar, and cereal), put them in a Ziploc plastic storage bag to protect from spillage and bugs that could get into your box during transit. If you are packing unopened glass food containers, also put these items in Ziploc bags. This way, if glass items get broken by accident, the damage will be contained in the plastic bag and will not affect the entire box of goods. Canned and dried foods may be shipped, but if they are lost or damaged, you may not be reimbursed by the moving company.

13. If you don't want to bring your plants, sell them, give them to friends and relatives, or ask your real estate agent if the new owner wants them. If plants are in expensive pots, you may want to dispose of the plants but keep the pots for future use. (Refer to Chapter Seven for more tips on how to help your plants survive during transit.)

14. Unscrew hoses and drain water from outdoor garden hoses before they are packed.

15. Disassemble furniture when possible. (If you have a water bed, drain the water. Then disassemble the bed, if necessary. A specialty services company may be hired to perform this job.)

16. Bring in small items from the yard that require packing. Identify any large items in the yard that need to be packed by the movers. (Refer to Chapter Six for gypsy moth inspection requirements.)

17. Packers bring all required materials to complete the entire packing process. They are required to use only new boxes and materials to keep your shipment sanitary.

18. Ask the packers to leave a few empty boxes, packing paper, and a roll of packing tape in case you find overlooked items after the packers and moving personnel have gone.

19. If you have a central vacuum system in your home, make sure the movers don't pack the vacuum hoses or accessories. Place these items in a box in the hall closet and mark "CENTRAL VACUUM SYSTEM—DO NOT LOAD ON TRUCK."

20. If you are moving long-distance, reconfirm the unloading date with your driver. If there is an unexpected delay in your unloading date caused by the moving company, you may be entitled to compensation for this change to your contract.

21. Leave your new address for the new owners so that they can forward any mail or items found in the house. (A friendly note and a large, postage-paid manila envelope with your new address would expedite this process.)

22. The following special services are not usually covered under a corporate relocation agreement unless specialty services are authorized under your agreement. If you are personally responsible for the packing bill, the more you can do yourself, the more money you will save.

    ■ Picking up and delivering items located at a place other than the current or new residence

    ■ Temporary storage of household items beyond a specified number of days (Review your contract for the exact number of days.)

    ■ Housecleaning, maid service, removal and installation of rugs and drapes

    ■ Disassembly of swing sets, portable swimming pools, hot tubs, light fixtures, ceiling fans, air conditioners, draining water beds and fish tanks, etc

    ■ Any item requiring the services of an electrician, carpenter, plumber or other special service (e.g., disconnecting a gas dryer and ice maker)

    ■ Temporary storage of your motor vehicle

CHAPTER NINE

Moving Day

Moving day has finally arrived. It seems like it has taken forever to get to this moment. This day is always a blur in my mind. There is so much activity that the day flies by all too quickly. It is an exhausting day, even more so if you are doing all of the loading yourself. The many useful tips in this chapter will help you get through moving day without losing control of the situation and getting frustrated.

Be Ready Bright and Early

Introduce yourself, your family, and your pets to the moving personnel when they arrive. Since moving companies like to get started early, make sure someone is home to meet the movers and point out which items are to be loaded onto the truck. Clearly identify any items that should not be loaded on the truck, and put them in a special place with a visible sign labeled "DO NOT LOAD." Put a "LOAD LAST" sign on the following items: vacuum cleaner, broom, ladder, survival box, packed suitcases, box of shoes, etc.

Give the driver and the crew a tour of the house and yard when they arrive. Show them the way around your property and tell them about any special items that are *not* to be loaded onto the truck. This is a good time to ask questions about the loading of your furniture and boxes. Note that the driver is the person in charge of the move. Go directly to him or her if you need any help on moving day.

Get plenty of rest the night before moving. Moving day is the most stressful day of all in the moving process. Even though the movers usually plan on having the truck loaded by 5:00 or 6:00 P.M., the job can take longer due to inclement weather or unforeseeable events. Therefore, it's best to plan on the job taking several more hours than scheduled. If you are moving out of town and traveling by airplane, stay in a hotel on moving night and fly to your destination the following day. If the truck's loading schedule is delayed, you will avoid penalties associated with changing your travel arrangements.

Reputable moving companies will place moving pads, mats, cardboard, or clear plastic on the entrance floors, in the hallways, and on the stairs. Pads should be hung over railings to prevent damage.

If you are not able to get a babysitter and must have small children at the house on moving day, remember to keep children safe. This means out of the truck, off the truck platform, and away from heavy items being moved. Children can be seriously injured if they are running around and playing in unsupervised areas. Keep them safe by providing strict rules about where they can play on moving day.

Put your pets in a secure place so that they do not get hurt or lost on moving day. Dogs and cats should be wearing their identification collars.

Being prepared on moving day can save you time, money, and energy and make this hectic day less stressful.

Specialty Services

In most corporate moves, a special services employee will come to your old house and, later, to your new house to perform the following specialty services:

Disconnecting and Connecting Service

- Washer
- Dryer
- Ice maker
- Other _____

Disassembly and Assembly Service

- Grandfather or grandmother clock
- Pool table
- Swing set

- Water bed
- Wall unit
- Exercise equipment
- Light fixtures

Piano Service

Piano service personnel will prepare and properly wrap your piano and bench for loading.

Wooden Crating Service

- Glass-top tables
- Large mirrors
- Delicate artwork

Movers Specialty Service, Inc. and Craters & Freighters are both specialty service companies that have done an outstanding job for me. They work in many different states. They can be reached at:

Movers Specialty Service, Inc.
211 Commerce Drive
Montgomeryville, PA
(800) 433–1159

Craters & Freighters
7000 East Forty-seventh Avenue
18936 Denver, CO 80216
(800) 736–3335

Martha's Moving Survival Tips

Truck drivers hate bugs. I once heard a story from a truck driver about a woman's house that was so infested with bugs that he refused to move her. State regulations dictate that moving vans must be kept clean and sanitary. If you have cockroaches or other bugs in your house, or gypsy moth larva on outdoor plants or equipment, have them exterminated before moving day. Then you won't infest the moving van, your new house, or the environment.

Time to Start Cleaning

If you have not hired a cleaning professional, then you can begin the cleaning process as each room is emptied.

1. Make sure the vacuum cleaner and your box of cleaning products are labeled appropriately so that they are not put on the truck until you are finished cleaning.

2. Vacuum and wipe out all cabinets, drawers, and closets.

3. Vacuum the carpets and floors. Wash the floors if necessary.

4. When the refrigerator and washer and dryer are moved, the floor will usually require cleaning. Be prepared to scrub the floor using old rags or a mop.

5. Sweep out the basement and garage.

6. After the house is empty, you will probably have rubbish to dispose of. Place the rubbish in your trash can, or put the rubbish in an extra moving box.

7. Leave a cordial note for the new homeowners asking them to kindly put out the rubbish on garbage day. (Identify which day of the week the garbage collector is scheduled to come.) If you are leaving your trash can for the new owners, include in the note that you have donated the trash can to them.

Tips for Handling Your Own Move

If you are handling your own move with the help of friends, organize the loading to maximize space in the truck and to ensure that heavy boxes do not get loaded onto boxes of breakables. Load your survival box and kitchen boxes toward the back of the moving van so that they can be removed first for immediate access. Carefully monitor the loading process: Friends have good intentions, but they won't be familiar with what is in each box. Make sure boxes are not dropped or thrown onto the truck.

During the loading and unloading process, keep an ample supply of food and beverages for the movers and yourself to keep everyone's spirits and energy level elevated.

Refer to Chapter Seven for special packing techniques and a list of items requiring special handling on moving day.

Double-check the House

Make sure all of your belongings are loaded in the moving van before the driver departs. Your phone, vacuum cleaner, broom, ladder, and survival box should be loaded last. Recheck the following places to make sure nothing has been left behind:

- Closets, drawers, cabinets, and medicine cabinets
- Dishwasher, oven, and microwave
- Attic, basement, and garage
- Balcony, yard, toolshed, porch, greenhouse

Martha's Moving Survival Tips

The moving snafu. It had been an extremely hectic moving day and the moving van was not loaded until 9:00 P.M. It was a school night for my children, and we had to stay at a local hotel for the night. I didn't have time to examine every drawer in the house before the moving van pulled away. The next morning I discovered an entire drawer full of unpacked bathroom items. Hmm . . . what to do? I decided to mail the supplies to my new house. A few weeks later I wrote a letter to the mover's claims department requesting payment for the shipment of the forgotten items. Since I had to ship these items due to negligence on the part of the moving company, they reimbursed me for these charges. However, the moving company is only authorized to provide reimbursement for expenses if the situation is explained in writing and the *original receipt* for the expense is included.

If anything is left in your house or apartment, it will be your responsibility to have it delivered to your new residence. Remove all picture hooks from the walls and touch up paint if necessary. Before the moving van departs, carefully check your home for possible property damage caused during the move. Inform the driver immediately if you notice any damage.

And last but not least:

- Turn off the lights, except one or two for security purposes.
- Close the blinds and draperies.
- Lock all doors, windows, and gates. Activate the security system if applicable.
- Adjust the automatic sprinkler system accordingly.
- Adjust the temperature on the thermostat for the heater or air conditioner.
- Encourage small children to say good-bye to the house, room by room!
- Say good-bye to friendly neighbors before you drive off.

If a relocation company is purchasing your house, check your relocation contract regarding the required condition of the house at departure. An assigned real estate agent will usually drop by to visually inspect the house as soon the moving van departs. Do not leave gasoline cans full of gas or oil in the garage or you could be billed by the relocation company (up to $100) to have them hauled away. (Gas or oil left in the garage of an unoccupied house is considered an insurance liability.) There may also be a cleaning charge imposed if your house is not left in satisfactory condition.

Driver's Bill of Lading Checklist

The bill of lading is the contract between you and the moving company and the only receipt for your belongings. It is also referred to as an inventory checklist. Study it carefully.

- Verify your insurance protection.
- Verify the delivery date and delivery address.
- Exchange cell phone or pager notification phone numbers with the driver.

■ Provide the driver with accurate, written directions to your new location.

■ Let the driver know if your new property poses any unloading difficulties. If you live in a gated community, inform the gate personnel about the arrival of the moving van. If the gate is not staffed, you must be present to allow the van access into the area.

■ Make sure both you and the driver sign the bill of lading. It is *your* responsibility to read and understand this document before signing it. Once the bill of lading is signed, it becomes a legally binding contract.

■ Keep a signed copy of the bill of lading with you. Place it in your box of personal belongings that will not be loaded onto the moving van. You will need his paperwork to verify your shipment at your destination and to serve as documentation in case you have to file a claim for damaged or missing goods.

■ To the best of your ability, verify that all of your boxes and furniture have been tagged with a numbered sticker. The stickers ensure that your belongings are not mixed up with someone else's if the truck picks up another load before delivering your items, or if your belongings are put in storage. Each piece of furniture should be individually listed and its condition accurately described according to the code that is stated on the inventory sheet. Review all of the codes attributed to your furniture. Do they state or overstate scratches and dents in your furniture? Make sure you are in agreement with the codes assigned to your belongings.

■ The bill of lading may also serve as the freight bill (that is, the total cost of the shipment, plus the date and method of payment).

Ten Money-Saving Tips

When you have to pay for the move yourself, the following tips will help you save time, which will make your move less expensive and less frustrating.

1. Provide the driver with accurate directions that spell out the fastest route to your new location. (Refer to the Four Days to Go section of Chapter Eight for instructions.)

2. Locate keys to storage cabinets, storage facilities, gates, and doors.

3. Premeasure: Make sure your furniture will fit through the door or a window in your new location. Measure the space where you intend to put a piece of furniture to ensure that it will fit properly.

4. Tell the movers how furniture and appliances were originally brought into the house. This will prevent the movers from backtracking with heavy furniture to take another approach.

5. Disassemble large pieces of furniture yourself (such as beds, cribs, tables, and bookcases). Also disassemble Ping-Pong tables, basketball stands, floor lamps, hat stands, train sets, children's plastic play equipment, exercise equipment, and swing sets. Bring in the outdoor thermometer, flagpole holder, bird feeder, rain gauge, and any items that are outside. (These items can be easily forgotten in the rush of moving day.)

6. Temporarily remove doors from their hinges to allow large pieces of furniture or appliances to pass through more easily. Buy metal S hooks to shorten chains so that people don't hit their heads on chandeliers when removing furniture from beneath them.

7. Reserve the freight elevator at your new residence, if necessary.

8. Don't move anything that you will never use again!

9. If moving yourself, rent a dolly to move large boxes, furniture, pianos, and appliances. (Refer to Chapter Seven for special handling instructions for pianos and large appliances.)

10. If you are moving locally, move fragile items, small boxes, and small pieces of furniture in your own vehicle.

CHAPTER TEN

Delivery Day . . .
and Unpacking

Congratulations! You have arrived at your new home and have the keys in your hands. Enjoy the moment! Your new life is beginning to take shape. Take time to get excited about your new place before the moving van arrives. Delivery day will be another really long, exhausting day, and you will need stamina to get through it. You have made it this far and are now prepared to get through the final stretch.

If it is affordable, it's a great idea to stay in a hotel the night after the truck delivers your belongings. Otherwise you will be in a panic to get the beds put together and find the bed linens and towels before nightfall.

After the sixth move, I finally decided that my family definitely needed to add more fun to this process. On our move to Scottsdale, we checked into the Princess Resort the night before the moving van arrived at our new house. We relaxed, swam, and enjoyed a delicious dinner. We felt like we were on vacation, not in the middle of a hectic cross-country move. The next morning my family woke up refreshed and ready to greet the moving personnel at our new house. This situation is in stark contrast to the first time I moved and spent the night sleeping on the floor with my two babies at a relative's house. Dream up your own idea of relaxing and see if you too can put more fun for the whole family into your move.

Examine Your New Residence

Complete the final walk-through checklist for your new house or apartment before you sign the final contract documents. This should take place before the movers arrive—the day before is ideal. Check to ensure your house systems (heating and air-conditioning, electricity, hot-water heater, telephone, and security system) and major appliances (stove and cooktop, oven, microwave, dishwasher, refrigerator, washer and dryer) are working properly. Make sure all of the keys and locks on the doors, windows, and gates function properly.

Make an initial survey of each room. Confirm that the place is in the condition stated in your contract or rental agreement. Now is the time to document any concerns regarding unexpected defects in your home or apartment. Call your landlord or real estate agent immediately if you notice problems. You could jeopardize your legal rights if defects are not reported promptly. If the house does not live up to your housekeeping standards, hire cleaning personnel or clean it up yourself.

Take the Driver on a Tour

Make sure you arrive to meet the movers at an agreed-upon time. Movers are under a tight schedule and need to get started promptly. If they are delayed due to your late arrival, you may be charged for their time even though they did not do work.

When the movers arrive, introduce yourself, your family, and your pets to the movers. The driver and moving personnel will want a tour of the new place to determine how to get the furniture through doorways and up and down staircases. The driver will decide where it is easiest to unload the truck. In some instances, a smaller truck will be used to shuttle furniture and boxes up and down steep or nar-

Martha's Moving Survival Tips

The moving van broke down. Fortunately, a moving van is made up of two parts, the cab and the trailer. If the driver has a problem with the engine, he can separate the cab from the trailer and get the engine repaired while the trailer is being loaded, or he can rent another cab to get your load to its destination on time. Truck drivers own their own vehicles. They take great pride in ownership and keep the trucks in tip-top condition. Breakdowns should be rare.

row driveways. Make sure moving pads are placed in the appropriate places again: on entrance floors, in hallways, on stairs, and over railings.

Once the unloading begins, it's important to locate your linen boxes as soon as possible so that you can make your bed after it's assembled and take a shower at the end of the day. Also locate your survival box.

Label the Rooms and Doors

To speed up the delivery process, write each occupant's name on a piece of paper and tape it to each bedroom wall or door. These names should match the identification names written on the packing boxes. If it's hard to differentiate the living room from the family room in the new location, put labels on these rooms also.

Why go to the trouble of labeling rooms? The movers will have to keep asking you which room is which if no signs direct them to the correct rooms. Or even worse, boxes and furniture will be placed in the wrong location, which will greatly complicate unpacking.

If you notice that a heavy box has been placed in the incorrect room despite your signs and labels, ask the movers to carry it to its correct location so that you will not have to do this yourself later.

Post Furniture Arrangements

If you would like furniture arranged in a particular way, draw the layout of your furniture on an 8½ x 11 inch sheet of paper. Tape the paper to the wall just outside the entrance to the room so the movers will see it before they enter the room. If a furniture layout is not provided, and if you are not available to direct the movers, then they will arrange the furniture as they see fit. That may not be the way you like it!

At the very least, have a general idea of a furniture arrangement. Movers usually don't mind relocating a piece of furniture once, but they will be too busy to move it from room to room if you repeatedly change your mind about the location. Note too that extremely bulky and heavy items can only be moved once.

Make sure all unassembled furniture is put back together correctly, even if the unpacking will be done the next day. It is the mover's job to reassemble furniture the same day it is delivered to your new location (unless, of course, you are trying to save money and have planned to do the reassembly yourself).

Supervise Your Children and Pets

Moving can be traumatic for children and pets too! It is extremely important to keep children supervised during the unloading process. Make sure that you have snacks and drinks available for youngsters.

Young children may be frightened the first few nights in your new home. To make them feel more secure, make sure they know the way from their room to the master bedroom. Then if they come looking for you in the middle of the night for comfort, they will not get disoriented or scared.

Supervise your pets too. Introduce your dog to its new environment, both inside and outside the yard area. If you have an outdoor cat, make sure it's safe to let it outside, especially at night. Give your pets food and water, and make sure they feel comfortable and safe in their new surroundings so that they do not run away.

Show Compassion for Moving Personnel

Be considerate! Have cold bottles of water and beverages for your movers, regardless of whether they are professionals or volunteers, especially during warm weather. It's a good idea to have your telephone plugged in immediately (or have a cellular phone available) to order food or call for help in case of emergency. If the moving personnel did not bring their lunch, you may want to offer to buy lunch for them. Pizza is always a good choice.

Refer to the Inventory Checklist

You will need to have in hand your inventory checklist (the driver's bill of lading checklist) before anything is unloaded from the moving van. Check off each inventory numbered item on the list as the movers carry it into your house. It's easier to keep track of your inventory if two people are available to help. One person can check off the inventory while the other person makes sure the boxes and furniture are placed in the correct location. If you are by yourself, you will have to perform both tasks simultaneously (that is, check off each numbered item as it is brought into the house and direct the item to the correct location). If your belongings fill the entire truck, this step can be eliminated as long as you trust the moving company.

Make a notation on the inventory list of any missing or damaged inventory, and review the list with the driver before he leaves your job. If there are missing items or boxes, the moving company will try to locate them by the numbered stickers on the items. If your belongings are not found, you will be required to fill out a claim form listing the item number and contents of the box with an appropriate replacement value. If you have damaged inventory, you will also list it on this form.

The driver will ask you to sign or initial the inventory list at the bottom of each page before he leaves. For your protection, sign each sheet and write "subject to inspection" so that you can inspect each item within the allotted time period. If you believe that an item may have been stolen, contact the moving company immediately, file a police report, and inform your insurance agent of the problem.

In accordance with the Department of Transportation's rules and regulations, you have nine months from the date of delivery to file your claim in writing with the carrier. However, the moving company will encourage you to file your claim within ninety days of delivery. It is your job to make sure the claim form is filled out accurately, signed in the designated places, and mailed to the correct address. Carefully check *all* of your boxes and furniture to make sure there was no other damage caused during transit before sending in the claim form.

💡 Martha's Moving Survival Tips

The driver of the year award. Drivers do not like to travel with an empty or partially loaded truck because they make more money with a full load. During slow times of the year, drivers may wait a few extra days for a full load. I was lucky enough to have this situation happen to my driver on one of my moves. His name is Bubba, and to this day I am thankful for his help.

The moving company was having trouble locating an unpacking crew, and I was going to have to wait two or three days to get my belongings unpacked. My husband was out of town on a business trip, and I had a four-year-old daughter and five-year-old son to contend with. Unpacking was going to be quite an ordeal by myself. Then Bubba volunteered to do all of the unpacking himself, with my assistance. He decided that it would be more productive to earn additional money unpacking instead of just waiting around Seattle for another job. As he unpacked every box, I put everything away in the cabinets and on the shelves. He even helped me organize the heavy boxes in the garage. By the end of the second day, the entire house was unpacked and our two cars fit in the garage. This was by far the best move I have ever had, and I believe Bubba deserves an award for his outstanding service.

If you find a damaged item, you must keep it so that the insurance adjuster can identify the item and make the decision to repair or replace it. If you dispose of the object before the insurance adjuster visually inspects it, you will lose your legal right to reimbursement.

If the item must be replaced, the adjuster will assign an equitable value to that object and the moving company will reimburse you according to the assigned amount. The exception is when you have an appraisal document or a receipt authenticating a higher value.

If the item requires repair, someone from a repair company will be sent to your house to fix the object on the premises or to take it to a shop for repair. The repair company will be responsible for returning to your home any items that it removes.

Check for Damage during the Move In

Before the moving van departs, make sure that the movers have not caused any damage to your new residence (such as scratched woodwork or dented walls) as they were moving furniture and boxes into the house. Report damage to the driver immediately.

Call Family and Friends

After your move in is complete and the moving van has departed, call your family and friends to let them know that you have arrived safely. It will be exciting to tell someone about your new place, and hearing a familiar voice will make you feel more comfortable in your new surroundings.

Receiving Your Vehicle

When your vehicle arrives at its final destination, compare the condition of your vehicle with the description on the transport documents. Make this condition check during daylight hours. Your car will probably be very dirty if it traveled on an open car-carrier truck. It is best to get it washed before conducting the final examination of its condition.

If the condition of your vehicle is acceptable, sign the transport documents to indicate that you are satisfied with its condition. If you cannot conduct a proper inspection at the time of delivery, indicate in writing on the transport documents that a proper inspection has not taken place. Then check your vehicle over very carefully the following day. If any damage has occurred, document the defects in writing on the transport documents and call your moving coordinator immediately. Follow the explicit instructions provided to you to get the damage repaired expeditiously.

Supervising the Unpacking Crew

Check your contract to determine if unpacking services are authorized. If so, it's important to request unpacking personnel in advance. Depending on your specific situation, the moving company may send an unpacking crew on moving day or wait until the following day to unpack. If unpacking will take place on moving day, keep in mind that your house will be very disorganized when the unpacking is complete. The unpackers, job is *only* to unpack. They take everything out of your boxes and lay the items down on the floor, on a countertop, or on a piece of furniture. They take your clothes out of the wardrobe boxes and hang them in the closet. (Make sure the wardrobe boxes are in their correct rooms or you will have your clothes hanging in the wrong closet.) In most cases it's preferable to have the movers start unpacking on the day *after* the move in.

You will want to have your refrigerator, ice maker, and washer and dryer hooked up immediately by the specialty service company.

To minimize the disorganization caused by unpacking, you may want to designate certain boxes to be unpacked first:

Martha's Moving Survival Tips

Don't drop the dishes. Moving companies conserve resources by training unpackers to work as quickly as possible. However, there should be a happy medium between efficiency to make a profit and rushing so much that your valuables get broken. If you notice that the unpackers seem careless with your belongings, ask them to slow down and be more gentle when unpacking. Occasionally, an item will be broken by accident. This is only normal. But if you notice that *many* items are getting broken, you should be concerned! If the unpackers are not listening to your requests, call the moving company at once. Reputable moving personnel will try to resolve this situation expeditiously and to your satisfaction.

Survival box

Computer equipment and printer

Food and kitchen necessities

Linens and bathroom items

TV, VCR, and DVD player

Wardrobe boxes and clothing boxes

Telephone and answering machine

Lamps and plants

Stereo system and speakers

Video game player and video games

Home videos and DVDs

Tapes and CDs

You may want to unpack other boxes yourself, or you might ask if the unpackers can return in a few days to unpack the remaining boxes:

Books and toys

Sports and recreational equipment

China, glassware, and knickknacks

Specialty and seasonal items

Pictures, mirrors, and crated items

Tools, garage, and outdoor items

Removing Packing Materials

Request that the unpackers dispose of all packing materials and empty boxes from your house. (This may be referred to as a "debris pick-up.") In some instances, the unpackers may have to leave materials and boxes in your garage for a few days and come back with another truck to pick them up. The boxes may have to be broken down before being loaded onto a truck. This can be a time-consuming process if there are numerous boxes. Other times the driver loads the boxes back on the truck immediately.

If removing the debris is not included in your contract, break down the boxes yourself and dispose of them using your curbside recycling service or take them to your local recycling center. Alternatively, you can donate your boxes to friends who may be moving soon.

Crated Items and Appliance Hookups

If large mirrors, glass-top tables, or artwork was crated, a special services person will be sent to your house to uncrate them. This person will also hook up your refrigerator, ice maker, washer, and dryer. Special services cannot always be scheduled on moving day. You may have to wait from one to two days after your move-in date to receive this service.

Tips for Doing Your Own Unpacking

If you are doing your own unpacking and the job is large, don't try to unpack everything at once. Unpack in a logical fashion.

- Unpack your survival box. Plug in your alarm clock and coffee machine. Put toilet paper, soap, shampoo and cream rinse, and towels in the bathrooms immediately. Hang up the shower curtain if your bathroom needs one.

- Locate your lamps and lightbulbs. Plug in your lamps before it is too dark to see what you are doing.

- Hook up your telephone. Plug in your answering machine, or check to make sure your voice mail service has been activated.

- Hook up your television, stereo, and computer equipment. Hook up your refrigerator and washer and dryer (unless a specialty service company will do this job).

- Put your beds back together, unpack your linen boxes, and make the beds.

- Take a quick trip to the grocery store to pick up a few necessities.

- If you moved to a new time zone, reset your watch and automobile clock to the correct time in your new area.

- Find a place to store boxes that do not have to be unpacked immediately (garage, basement, attic, large closet, or vacant room). This will eliminate a lot of clutter and create room to unpack the remaining boxes.

- Unpack gingerly: Double-check every box to make sure that small items do not get thrown away with the packing paper. Handle fragile items carefully to prevent breakage during unpacking. Unpacking carefully, and in an organized manner, will save time and energy in the long run.

Refer to the suggested order of unpacking in the "Supervising the Unpacking Crew" section earlier in this chapter.

A Secret to Getting Your Kitchen Organized Fast

Put everything away as quickly as possible in a logical manner, but don't worry about final placement. If you have unpackers helping you, put items directly into a cabinet, drawer, or pantry as each item is taken out of the box and unwrapped. As soon as your kitchen is functional, you will not feel so overwhelmed! Then, after the unpackers are gone and the rest of your house is somewhat organized, you can begin rearranging your kitchen the way you want it to remain permanently.

Children Can Be Helpful Too!

If your children are old enough, let them help you unpack. Ask them to empty the boxes in their new room and find a special place for their belongings. Children love to organize their drawers and are proud to show you their hard work when finished. They will probably amaze you with their enthusiasm and creativity. By keeping children busy with their own projects, you will have more time to organize other areas of the house.

Martha's Moving Survival Tips

Not mine! As I was putting things away in my new kitchen, I came across a small teapot left by the previous owners. The owners were thoughtful enough to leave me their new address and a nice note about the new neighborhood. I immediately mailed the teapot to them, and I am sure they were thrilled to receive it. Be considerate and return any items that do not belong to you, or ask the real estate agent to do so. If you do not have the previous owners' address, call your agent to get it. It will only take a few minutes of your time, and a simple gesture such as this could really make someone's day better.

CHAPTER ELEVEN

Getting Your New Life on Track

Getting your new life on track is the key to making your move successful. The logistics of moving are now complete; next you have to find a way to assimilate into your new community. In addition, there are several legal tasks you must accomplish to keep you a law-abiding citizen. This chapter gives you explicit instructions to accomplish these tasks so that you can complete them before the deadline to avoid any unnecessary fines or collect any payments owed. You'll also find guidelines for locating competent doctors, dentists, and orthodontists in a new community. And don't forget to review the Comprehensive Moving Checklist in Appendix A and the worksheets in Appendix B to get your life back to normal more quickly.

Change Your Driver's License

The law specifies the amount of time you have to get a new driver's license (if you moved out of state) or to change your address (if you moved within your state). The following time periods may vary from state to state, so review your state's driver's manual for the specific rules.

- If your home address changed, report the address change in one week.
- For a legal name change (marriage or adoption), report the name change in two weeks.
- If you have an out-of-state license and move into a new state, apply for a new license within sixty days or before your current license expires, whichever is sooner.

Look in the community pages or newcomer's information section of your local telephone directory for the closest driver's license office. Call the telephone number listed for directions, hours of operation, and time-period requirements. The operator or a recording will tell you what you need to bring with you to get a new driver's license. You can ask your real estate or insurance agent for assistance in locating the nearest motor vehicle office. Or check the Internet for this information.

Some states require a written test if you are from out of state, while other states will renew a current license with a vision test and small fee. If you are getting your license for the first time, or your current license has been expired for more than three years, a road test will usually be required. Waiting lines in the motor vehicle office can be lengthy, so schedule your time accordingly.

You will need to show proof of age and identity. A current driver's license and a second legal document are often required. The following proofs are acceptable, listed in descending order of importance:

- Original U.S. birth certificate in English or a U.S. Department of State birth certificate with U.S. consulate seal
- Certified copy of U.S. birth certificate
- Active or expired U.S. passport
- Valid foreign passport (with current, acceptable I-94 form)
- Valid U.S. alien registration card or valid work authorization card, combined with a Social Security card or a U.S. certificate of naturalization
- U.S. citizenship papers
- U.S. military identification card (active duty only); no dependent cards or military discharge papers (DD-214)
- U.S. adoption papers with proof of legal presence in the United States
- Original legal name change papers, civil marriage or divorce documents, or certified copy of the same with proof of legal presence in the United States

■ Any other document issued by the U.S. government that establishes the applicant's proof of identity and date of birth and verifies that the applicant's presence in the United States is authorized under federal laws

If your surname is different from the one on your primary proof of age and identity, you must provide documentation for the name change. Name changes through divorce must be part of the divorce decree or contain an addendum signed by the hearing judge.

■ Marriage, adoption or divorce certificate. (Must be original or certified copy with the state or municipal seal.)
■ Name change court order.

Change Your License Plates

You typically have sixty days (or less if your out-of-state registration expires before then) after you move to a new state to apply for a new title and register your vehicle.

Look in the community pages or newcomer's information section of your local telephone directory for the closest motor vehicle office in your county. Call the telephone number listed for directions and hours of operation. The operator or a recording will tell you what documentation you will need to get new license plates. Don't forget to register your recreational vehicles!

Martha's Moving Survival Tips

Registering your vehicle can get tricky. When registering your motor vehicle in a new state, you will need the title, lease agreement, or lien-holder documentation. If two parties are listed on the title (husband and wife, for example), both parties must sign the title and registration application before the vehicle can be registered. If the vehicle is leased, you must request a power of attorney from the automobile dealer before the vehicle can be registered in another state. In most states, your car will need to pass an emissions test if the vehicle is more than three years old, and a vehicle identification inspection will be required before the car can be registered.

Bring required documents and cash or a check to pay any required fees. Typical required documentation includes:

- Current vehicle registration form
- Current title (original document of certificate of title)
- Proof of insurance
- Valid driver's license from the state in which you are registering the vehicle

Different states have different inspection rules. Safety inspections, emission inspections, and vehicle identification number (VIN)) verifications may be required within a specific time period before a new license plate or an automobile insurance policy will be issued. In some states, such as California, your local American Automobile Association (AAA) office is authorized to issue new license plates. In other states, such as New Jersey, the insurance company requires a photo inspection and a copy of a utility bill documenting residence in the state before an insurance policy will issued.

Change Your Voter Registration

Look in the government pages section of your telephone directory for instructions on how to register to vote. There will be a number listed to call for further information. The registration form must be postmarked, or delivered in person, at least twenty-nine days before the next election if you are to qualify to vote on election day.

In most states, residents may register to vote at the following places:

- Department of motor vehicles or motor vehicle services
- Voter registration office or public assistance agency
- Public library or many other public and private offices in your community
- Over the Internet at www.homeadvisor.msn.com
- By mail on an approved form available from any county clerk's office

Get a New Library Card

You must have a current driver's license or some form of identification (student identification, utility bill, etc.) from your new state to get a library card. Students can get a library card too. To find the library closest to you, look in the community pages or newcomers information section of your telephone directory.

You can locate important information about your new community at your local library. If you are conserving resources, remember that borrowing library books and videos is free, unless of course they are not returned on time. Small children love to explore their local library and discover new books. Libraries often have children's story time on specific days. Computers with Internet connections may be available at your local library if you need this service.

File a Claim

If any of your inventory is damaged or missing, you will have to file a claim to request repair of the item, or to be eligible for monetary reimbursement. Call the moving company immediately, and request a claim form. Fill it out completely, sign it, and mail it to the correct address as soon as you have surveyed your entire inventory.

You usually have ninety days (check your contract for the specific number of days) to send in a claim form. After the official time period, the moving company will not be held legally responsible for repair or reimbursement of any items. If you do not hear from the moving company within a reasonable amount of time after submitting your claim, do not hesitate to call them regarding its status.

Filing a claim often seems like a nuisance after all of the work it took to get moved and settled. It is also a step that is sometimes forgotten in the scramble to move on with your life. However, such claims can often result in equitable compensation owed to you. I recommend that you carefully review your inventory and file a claim before the deadline if you find that any items are missing or damaged. Each time you find a damaged item, add it to the list in Appendix B so that you don't forget to claim it.

You'll find additional information about filing claims in Chapter Ten.

Locate Doctors, Dentists, and Orthodontists

It been said that people will spend more time picking out a car than they spend choosing a physician or a school for their child. Why is this? Because picking out a car is fun, but choosing a doctor or a new school can be a time-consuming, difficult challenge. However, since choosing a doctor could one day mean the difference between life and death, and choosing a school could mean the difference between career success and failure, it's important to spend some time on these decisions.

Finding a New Doctor

1. Choose a physician who graduated from an American or Canadian medical school. Both countries uphold strict standards for accreditation.

2. Choose a physician who did his or her residency at a university teaching hospital. These institutions generally have excellent faculty, attract difficult cases, and produce highly qualified graduates.

3. Choose a physician that is National Board Certified. This shows that the doctor has passed exams in a designated specialty. To verify certification, call the American Board of Medical Specialties at (800) 776–2378, or go to www.abms.org.

4. If you have a choice between several HMO and PPO plans, review the list of physicians who participate in each plan. Then consider the number of doctors and specialists participating in each plan and their qualifications. Ask which hospitals are affiliated with each plan and what type of prescription drug plan is offered. Review the office location, monthly fees, out-of-pocket costs, and deductibles of each plan.

5. Ask other doctors, nurses, and patients whom you respect and trust for a referral. If your primary-care physician is located in a large medical building, he or she may refer you to other physicians in the building or in the vicinity when necessary.

6. The practitioner's personality and reputation also play a role in your decision making. Ask for recommendations from family members, friends, or neighbors. A good doctor always earns a good reputation.

7. Call the chief of internal medicine at a local hospital and ask for a referral. The chief resident is always the best qualified and will usually be flattered at your request.

8. Browse the Internet to locate a new doctor, dentist, or chiropractor in your community. Log on to www.locateadoc.com, bestdoctors.com, or ama-assn.org.

9. Call ASK–A–NURSE or visit your local hospital and ask a few clinical nurses for a recommendation. Nurses work with doctors every day and know their personalities, competencies, and idiosyncrasies.

10. Call each practice and ask about approved insurance plans, payment options, location, and office hours, and if they are accepting new patients.

11. Before making your final decision, interview several doctors. If a doctor is not willing to be interviewed, you may want to choose someone else. A face-to-face interview will reveal much about personality, medical style, and competency. Ask the physicians for the names of the hospitals at which they have admitting privileges and to which colleagues patients are referred. Some doctors don't bill patients for initial interviews, while others charge a small fee or the full price of a regular visit. Consider this extra expense worthwhile if it results in a long-term relationship with a caring, competent doctor.

12. The doctor should be understanding and listen to your needs. Trust your gut instincts. If the office or the doctor does not feel right, move on in the interviewing process and find one who suits your standards, personality, and medical needs. It is easier to find a good doctor if you eliminate the inappropriate ones.

13. If your doctor seems impaired by drugs or alcohol, beware! Approximately 10 percent of the nation's physicians have problems with substance abuse. In addition, approximately 2 percent have a criminal record or other infractions. If you are concerned about a physician's behavior, visit www.docboard.org, questionabledoctors.org, quackwatch.com, or docinfo .org, to learn more about unethical or questionable doctors.

Finding a New Dentist

Finding the right dentist is another arduous task. The yellow pages will usually have a section called "Dentist Information Bureau" that lists many dentists' referral services, such as 1–800–DENTIST. Call the referral service and ask for a recommendation in your neighborhood. Internet sites for locating dentists include www .smileworks.com and www.locateadoc.com. If you have an HMO dental plan, you will be able to choose from a list of dentists in the plan. It's a good idea to interview potential dentists just as you would a doctor. Visit their offices and ask about the dentists' credentials, insurance carriers, payment options, and office hours and if they are accepting new patients. Ask how they handle emergencies and referrals for specialists. Follow the same rules you would use for finding a competent doctor.

Finding a New Orthodontist

You may want to follow the same steps that you use for finding a competent dentist. However, if you find a dentist first, he or she will usually recommend several orthodontists in the area. If you or your children are in the middle of orthodontic treatment, you will need to have your records and impressions transferred. Set up an initial consultation with each orthodontist you are considering, and bring to each appointment your records, impressions, and orthodontic appliances such as headgear and retainers. New panoramic X-rays may need to be taken by the orthodontist. An estimate for the treatment and treatment procedures should be completed by the end of the consultation. When you have made the final choice, schedule your first visit and return your records and impressions to the orthodontist office for its files.

Arrange for the Transfer of Medical Records

Arrange for the transfer of medical records to your new physician. Call your dentist to transfer records and those dental X-rays taken within the last two years to avoid extra medical expense and the discomfort of having them retaken. Women should request the transfer of their mammogram X-rays when they schedule their yearly appointment. If you move frequently, keep a list of all of the doctors and dentists you have seen in the past. Your new doctor may need to know the name of your former doctors, and you will want these names available in your records.

License Your Pets

City ordinances require the licensing of dogs and cats. The licensing form can usually be processed at your local municipal building or through the mail. A proof of rabies vaccination, proof of neutering or spaying, and fee should also be submitted with the form.

The Comprehensive Moving Checklist

The Comprehensive Moving Checklist is the master list that I refer to every day during a move. Many of the items listed in this checklist are referred to elsewhere in the moving guide. However, this list spells out every nitty-gritty moving detail that must be completed in most moves. I refer to this list up to one year after a move to make sure that every item is completed and to ensure I have not overlooked something significant that will come back to haunt me.

This list is divided into functional categories to make it easy to use. When an action is initiated, check off the first column labeled "Requested." Then when the action is completed, check off the second column labeled "Completed."

Notification of Change of Address

Send a change-of-address or a service-cancellation letter to the businesses listed below. Include your new telephone number in this correspondence. You confirm that an item has been completed when you receive the next issue, a monthly statement, or a bill with your new address printed correctly on the form.

	Requested	Completed
Post office (pick up change-of-address kit)	_____	_____
Magazines (six to eight weeks' notice required)	_____	_____
Newspapers (if moving locally)	_____	_____
Businesses	_____	_____
Emergency roadside service provider	_____	_____
Department of motor vehicle	_____	_____
Voter registration	_____	_____
Insurance agent	_____	_____
Credit card accounts	_____	_____
Debtors (bank, auto loan, etc.)	_____	_____
Airline mileage accounts	_____	_____
Bank and/or credit union	_____	_____
Professional organizations	_____	_____
Accountants	_____	_____
Brokerage and investment accounts	_____	_____
Lawyers	_____	_____
Employer	_____	_____
Tax assessor office	_____	_____
Social Security administration	_____	_____
Internal Revenue Service	_____	_____
Civic and social newsletters	_____	_____
Relatives, friends, and business associates	_____	_____
Church	_____	_____
Schools	_____	_____
Day-care facility	_____	_____
Clubs	_____	_____
Medical insurer (medical, dental, vision)	_____	_____
Medical board	_____	_____
Doctors	_____	_____
Optometrist	_____	_____

	Requested	Completed
Dentists and orthodontist	_____	_____
Cosmetics consultant	_____	_____
Veterinarian	_____	_____
Rental agency (furniture, costume, instrument rentals, etc.)	_____	_____
Address change on luggage tags	_____	_____

Cancel and Add Utilities

Provide the desired shutoff and turn-on dates and provide your new address for final billing. Request a refund of your deposit, if applicable. Do not have your utilities disconnected at your current residence until the day after you move out. Request that the utilities in your new residence be turned on the day before you move in. (Refer to Appendix B for connecting and disconnecting utilities worksheets.)

Request a new telephone number before you cancel your old number. You may ask that your new telephone number be given on the recorded message that announces that your old number has been disconnected. Remember to ask the phone company to list (or not to list) your new address and phone number in the local telephone directory. Tell them how you want the directory listing to read.

Request that electric, gas, heating, and water utility services be transferred to the new occupant or relocation company, not disconnected (unless the house will not be occupied by another person or will be winterized or demolished after you vacate the premises).

Tip: It is best to call early in the morning or late in the evening to avoid waiting on hold for an extended period of time.

	Requested	Completed
Telephone (request new phone number first)	_____	_____
Electric	_____	_____
Cable service	_____	_____
Gas	_____	_____
Heating	_____	_____
Sewer	_____	_____

	Requested	Completed
Water	_____	_____
Garbage collector	_____	_____
Security system monitoring service	_____	_____
Internet service provider	_____	_____
Voice mail service	_____	_____
Cellular phone service (transfer when possible to avoid cancellation charges)	_____	_____
Pager (if leaving the activation area)	_____	_____

Cancel and Reorder
Home Deliveries and Services

	Requested	Completed
Child-care provider	_____	_____
Dairy service	_____	_____
Diaper service	_____	_____
Dry-cleaning service	_____	_____
Exterminator	_____	_____
Fuel oil delivery service	_____	_____
Grocery delivery service	_____	_____
Home nursing care	_____	_____
Housecleaning service	_____	_____
House maintenance service	_____	_____
Lawn care service	_____	_____
Lawn maintenance service	_____	_____
Lawn winterizing service	_____	_____
Medical services provider	_____	_____
Music teacher	_____	_____
Newspaper delivery	_____	_____
Pet sitter and pet grooming	_____	_____

	Requested	Completed
Pool maintenance service		
Pool opening and closing service		
Snow removal service		
Tutors		
Water delivery service		
Water softener service		
Miscellaneous		
Miscellaneous		

Banking and Financial Issues

	Requested	Completed
Secure financing for your new home.		
Schedule new-house appraisal.		
Renters: Obtain funds for first and last months' rent and security deposit.		
Request wire transfer instructions.		
Close out and reopen safe-deposit box.		
Locate a new bank, saving and loan, or credit union.		
Inquire about automatic transfer of personal banking services from your current bank.		
Cancel direct deposits or automatic payments.		
Order checks with your new address and phone number.		
Apply for new ATM cards.		
Renters: Obtain security deposit refund.		

Insurance

	Requested	Completed
Get new insurance quotes or transfer current coverage.	_____	_____

This includes insurance for life, automobile, motorcycle, watercraft, RV, airplane, home, apartment, medical, etc. For recommendations, ask your relocation coordinator, your company's benefits program coordinator, or your financial advisor. Or check the Internet at www.quote smith.com. (Refer to Appendix B for homeowner's and auto insurance worksheets.)

	Requested	Completed
Cancel your current homeowner's insurance.	_____	_____

(Do this *after* your new policy is in effect and you have properly inspected your shipment for missing or damaged items.)

	Requested	Completed
Cancel insurance policies no longer required.	_____	_____

Return Rented and Borrowed Equipment

	Requested	Completed
Cable television box(es) and remote control(s)	_____	_____
Piano and/or instrument(s)	_____	_____
Computer equipment	_____	_____
Furniture and clothing	_____	_____
Recreational and sports equipment	_____	_____
Telephone(s)	_____	_____
Library books	_____	_____
Videos, video games, and DVDs	_____	_____
Trash and recycle bins	_____	_____
Return any unwanted purchases to local stores.	_____	_____

Medical

	Requested	Completed
Refill necessary prescriptions. (Request extra refills.)	_____	_____
Transfer medical, dental, and other records.	_____	_____
Locate new doctor(s).	_____	_____
Obtain new medical card(s).	_____	_____
Check state laws regarding vaccinations and physical examinations for children if moving to a new state.	_____	_____
Obtain new prescription drug card(s).	_____	_____
Locate new pharmacy.	_____	_____
Locate new dentist(s)/orthodontist.	_____	_____
Locate new optometrist.	_____	_____
Locate new veterinarian.	_____	_____
Obtain medical and inoculation records for animals.	_____	_____
Locate the closest hospital.	_____	_____

Legal

	Requested	Completed
Review and sign real estate contract(s).	_____	_____
Accept/decline company buyout offer.	_____	_____
Offer valid from: __/__/__ to __/__/__.	_____	_____
Sign and notarize power of attorney documents.	_____	_____
Send homeowner's manual to the relocation company.	_____	_____
Verify the amount and due date of your tax bill.	_____	_____
Settle any outstanding bills and debts (legal, private schools, loans, clubs, etc.).	_____	_____
Update your will or living trust if necessary.	_____	_____
Schedule house closing date(s).	_____	_____

	Requested	Completed
Selling House:		
Date: _____		
Time: _____		
Place: _____		
Buying House:		
Date: _____		
Time: _____		
Place: _____		
Wire transfer new-house closing funds.	_____	_____
Correct required items on home inspection list.	_____	_____
Schedule final walk-through on new house.	_____	_____
Hand over house, club, pool, gate, and mailbox keys to your real estate agent.	_____	_____
Provide garage door openers and/or security code to open garage doors to your agent.	_____	_____
Provide house security system code to your agent.	_____	_____
Bring closing papers from sale of current home to new home closing, if necessary.	_____	_____
Obtain final HUD-1 settlement statement.	_____	_____
Obtain new title policy and property deed.	_____	_____

House Inspections

Schedule house inspections as required. (Request a house walk-through checklist from your real estate agent or obtain a copy from a Web site.)

	Requested	Completed
General	_____	_____
Structural	_____	_____
Septic system and well	_____	_____
Radon	_____	_____

Pest/termite	_____	_____
Toxic mold	_____	_____
Pool/spa	_____	_____
Fire department: carbon monoxide and smoke detectors	_____	_____

Club Memberships

Transfer membership to your new location (if possible) to avoid forfeiting your deposit. Inquire to find out if any of your deposit is refundable or if your membership is transferable to a new location or if it can be sold to a new member. Cancel current memberships and join new clubs *after* you move.

	Requested	Completed
Health club	_____	_____
Country club	_____	_____
Tennis club	_____	_____
Golf club	_____	_____
Garden club	_____	_____
Other clubs	_____	_____

School

	Requested	Completed
Request school records transfer form.	_____	_____
Request, complete, and return school registration form.	_____	_____
Schedule children's school medical checkups.	_____	_____
Complete school bus transportation form.	_____	_____
Obtain copies of children's birth certificates.	_____	_____
Obtain state inoculation requirements.	_____	_____

Licenses and Registrations

	Requested	Completed
Apply for a new driver's license, or submit a change of address if you moved in state.	_____	_____
Get new vehicle license plates and/or notify the motor vehicle department of your new address.	_____	_____
Register to vote, or update your voter registration address if you moved in state.	_____	_____
Inquire about regulations, licenses, tags, and the transporting of pets.	_____	_____
Apply for or renew your medical license.	_____	_____
Apply for or renew your boating license.	_____	_____
Apply for or renew your fishing license.	_____	_____
Apply for or renew your hunting license.	_____	_____
Place your new automobile insurance identification cards in automobile and discard expired cards.	_____	_____

Items to Pick Up

	Requested	Completed
Laundry, dry cleaning, and/or alterations	_____	_____
Furs from special storage	_____	_____
Photos from the photo store	_____	_____
Shoes from the repair shop	_____	_____
Items from storage or self-storage facility	_____	_____
Any pending orders:	_____	_____
Framing	_____	_____
Furniture	_____	_____
Layaway items	_____	_____
Repairs	_____	_____
Miscellaneous	_____	_____
Any loaned items	_____	_____

Reimbursable Items

	Requested	Completed
Submit all applicable expenses and receipts to the relocation company for reimbursement.	_____	_____
Request a claim form for items lost or damaged in transit.	_____	_____
Fill out claim form completely and accurately.	_____	_____
Submit completed claim form before deadline. (Make copies of the form before mailing.)	_____	_____

New Residence

	Requested	Completed
Check to see if the house has been adequately cleaned.	_____	_____
Change the locks on the doors at new residence if the house was previously owned.	_____	_____
Get spare keys made to your new residence.	_____	_____
Reprogram security system code at new residence.	_____	_____
Apply for alarm user permit through your local police department (if required).	_____	_____
Reprogram code to your garage door keypad at new residence and/or reprogram garage code in automobile.	_____	_____
Measure room and window sizes in new house to plan for window covering and furniture arrangements.	_____	_____
If you moved into a gated community, call your homeowners' association and get your name added to the directory at the gate.	_____	_____
Call your homeowners' association to order a remote-control gate opener. (A fee may be required.)	_____	_____

Martha's Moving Survival Tips

Label your new community mailbox. If you have a community mailbox, it may be your responsibility to put your street address on the mailbox and obtain a mailbox key when you move in. If you aren't receiving mail, check to make sure this was done—before you call the post office. The mailman cannot deliver mail if your street number is not listed correctly on the mailbox.

Miscellaneous

	Requested	Completed
Drain sprinkler system (winterize when appropriate).	_____	_____
Drain gasoline and oil from gas-powered equipment:		
Lawn mower	_____	_____
Power trimmer	_____	_____
Snowblower or leaf blower	_____	_____
Motorcycle	_____	_____
Empty barbecue grill and camping stove fuel tanks.	_____	_____
Recycle appropriate items.	_____	_____
Hold a garage sale or donate unwanted items to charitable organizations.	_____	_____
Have automobile engine tuned, checked, and oil changed if moving long-distance.	_____	_____
Pack an extra copy of your telephone book.	_____	_____
Order or make new return-address labels.	_____	_____
Close out/reopen post office box.	_____	_____
Ask your real estate agent for the code to the lock box.	_____	_____
Cancel charge cards at local stores.	_____	_____
If you moved a piano, get it retuned.	_____	_____
Obtain a new library card.	_____	_____

	Requested	Completed
Inquire about regulations for moving plants.	_____	_____
Appraise antiques, jewelry, and valuable items.	_____	_____
Photograph or videotape high-value items.	_____	_____
Pack your survival box. (Refer to the list in Chapter Seven.)	_____	_____
Update profile for auto-rental club membership.	_____	_____
Purchase floor protectors for furniture legs.	_____	_____
Recaulk and touch up paint to cover holes in drywall.	_____	_____

Company Relocation Policy

	Requested	Completed
	_____	_____

Study your relocation agreement to identify what expenses are covered and which vendors and services are approved for your move. Also discuss insurance coverage levels for your belongings. You may need to purchase additional insurance if your relocation company does not provide an adequate amount to cover all of your possessions. Find out if the coverage levels are based on replacement value or price per pound. If the insurance is based on price per pound and you have not identified an item as "high value," you may not receive the full value for the item if you need to file an insurance claim.

Do not cancel your current homeowner's insurance policy until all of your belongings are safely moved to their new destination and examined for damage. You may be eligible for reimbursement through your current homeowner's insurance policy for any damage or replacement costs not covered by the moving company.

Call your moving coordinator if you need special assistance or have any questions or concerns. If the relocation company is located out of state, the staff should provide you with a toll-free number. It is their job to provide you with excellent assistance through this relocation process. If they are not available when you call, they should show prompt response by returning your phone call the following business day. If you feel that you are not getting satisfactory service from your assigned representative, ask to talk to the supervisor, or call your employer representative to clear up any issues that are confusing. It's extremely important to resolve minor problems as they occur and not wait until they adversely impact your move or emotional well-being.

Moving Details

Make sure the following concerns are addressed with your moving company/coordinator before your moving date.

	Requested	Completed
Moving date	_____	_____
Packing date(s)	_____	_____
Regulations affecting your shipment	_____	_____
Contract changes	_____	_____
Liability (insurance requirements)	_____	_____
Number of packers	_____	_____
Number of days to pack	_____	_____
Arrival time of packers	_____	_____
Number of movers	_____	_____
Arrival time of movers	_____	_____
Number of unpackers	_____	_____
Number of days to unpack	_____	_____
Arrival time of unpackers	_____	_____
Schedule crating/disconnecting services	_____	_____
Schedule uncrating/connecting services	_____	_____
Customer responsibilities	_____	_____
Tipping policy	_____	_____
Partial shipments	_____	_____
Shipment of motor vehicle(s)	_____	_____
Payment amount (if not paid by the relocation company)	_____	_____
Acceptable payment methods (except for most corporate transfers, payment is due in full at the end of the moving day)	_____	_____

_____ Cash   _____ Money order

_____ Certified check _____ Major credit card (sometimes accepted on an interstate move)

APPENDIX B

Relocation Worksheets

After moving so many times, I decided that I needed to keep all of my moving documents in one place. I was tired of scribbling notes on different sheets of paper and then trying to piece together all of the information so that I wouldn't misplace a contact phone number or forget to do something important. Thus I started to type worksheets to organize and keep my notes in one place so that I could carry this important information with me at all times.

Now, when my real estate agent or relocation counselor calls with a question, I can answer the question by referring to the worksheets even when I am away from home. I can get moving tasks accomplished as I wait in line at the DMV or at the doctor's office. As I drive by a local movie theater, health club, or a golf course, I jot down the address on my worksheet so that I remember where it is located when I try to find it again.

These worksheets have saved me an invaluable amount of time. When I get on the phone to connect or disconnect utilities, I have all of the information I need at my fingertips and I can get the job accomplished more quickly and efficiently. I use all of these forms before, during, and after my move to keep my life on track. You'll find them indispensable too!

Planning Calendar

Month: _____ Months to go: _____

Sunday	Monday	Tuesday	Wednesday	Thursday	Friday	Saturday
―	―	―	―	―	―	―
―	―	―	―	―	―	―
―	―	―	―	―	―	―
―	―	―	―	―	―	―
―	―	―	―	―	―	―

Planning Calendar

Month: _____ Months to go: _____

Sunday	Monday	Tuesday	Wednesday	Thursday	Friday	Saturday
___	___	___	___	___	___	___
___	___	___	___	___	___	___
___	___	___	___	___	___	___
___	___	___	___	___	___	___
___	___	___	___	___	___	___

Planning Calendar

Month: _____ Months to go: _____

Sunday	Monday	Tuesday	Wednesday	Thursday	Friday	Saturday
——	——	——	——	——	——	——
——	——	——	——	——	——	——
——	——	——	——	——	——	——
——	——	——	——	——	——	——
——	——	——	——	——	——	——

Important Relocation Contacts

Current address _____

Current phone number _____

Nearest cross streets _____

Temporary Address _____

New phone number _____

Nearest cross streets _____

New Address _____

New phone number _____

Nearest cross streets _____

Selling real estate company _____

Agent _____

Assistant _____

Office phone _____

Cell phone _____

Buying real estate company _____

Agent _____

Assistant _____

Office phone _____

Cell phone _____

Escrow/title company _____

Escrow officer _____

Assistant _____

Office phone _____

Cell phone _____

Loan company _____

Loan officer _____

Toll-free phone number _____

Address _____

Moving company _____

Driver's name _____

Toll-free phone number _____

Driver's pager number _____

Relocation company _____

Relocation consultant _____

Toll-free phone number _____

Auto transport service _____

Driver's name _____

Toll-free phone number _____

Driver's pager or cell phone number _____

Attorney _____

Firm _____

Assistant _____

Phone _____

Address _____

Hotel name _____

Address _____

Toll-free phone number _____

Reservation date(s) _____

Confirmation number _____

Airline reservations* _____

Airline _____

Date _____

Flight number _____

Departure time _____

Arrival time _____

Rental car agency _____

Confirmation number _____

* If you purchase electronic tickets, you will have one fewer thing to worry about losing!

Airport shuttle/limousine service _____

Phone number _____

Pickup time _____

Confirmation number _____

Current insurance company _____

Agent's name _____

Office number _____

Current policy number _____

Coverage cancellation date _____

New insurance company _____

Agent's name _____

Office number _____

New Policy number _____

Coverage effective date _____

Spouse's/significant other's office _____

Company _____

Address _____

Office number _____

Cell phone or pager _____

Spouse's/significant other's office _____

Company _____

Address _____

Office number _____

Cell phone or pager _____

General inspection company _____

Contact name _____

Contact number _____

Address _____

Inspector _____Phone _____General _____

Inspector _____Phone _____Structural _____

Inspector _____Phone _____Septic/well _____

Inspector _____Phone _____Radon _____

Inspector _____Phone _____Pest/termite _____

Inspector _____Phone _____Toxic mold _____

Inspector _____Phone _____Pool/spa _____

Inspector _____Phone _____Fire Dept. _____

Appraisal company _____

Contact name _____

Toll-free phone number _____

New Emergency Telephone Numbers

Emergency (Ambulance—Fire—Police) . . . 911

Poison control _____

Animal control _____

Airport information _____

Road conditions _____

Emergency road service provider _____

Security system monitoring service _____

Hospital _____

Phone _____

Address _____

Directions _____

Pharmacy _____

Phone _____

Address _____

Medical insurance carrier _____

ID number _____

Phone _____

Doctors _____

Name _____   Phone _____

Address _____

Name _____   Phone _____

Address _____

Other Important New Numbers

Dentists _____

Name _____ Phone _____

Address _____

Name _____ Phone _____

Address _____

Child-care provider _____

Phone _____

Address _____

School _____

Phone _____

Address _____

Teacher _____

Teacher _____

School _____

Phone _____

Address _____

Teacher _____

Teacher _____

Church _____

Phone _____

Address _____

Babysitters _____

Name _____ Phone _____

Name _____ Phone _____

Veterinarian _____

Phone _____

Address _____

Bank/investment company _____

Phone _____

Address _____

Music teacher _____

Phone _____

Address _____

Dance/gymnastics/skating/art instruction _____

Phone _____

Address _____

Boy Scout troop no. _____ **Den no.** _____

Leader's name _____

Phone _____

Address _____

Girl Scout troop no. _____

Leader's name _____

Phone _____

Address _____

Health club facility/YMCA _____

Phone _____

Address _____

Sports program (Sport) _____

Phone _____

Address _____

Sports program (Sport) _____

Phone _____

Address _____

Golf course _____

Phone _____

Address _____

Auto mechanic _____

Phone _____

Address _____

Local post office _____

Phone _____

Address _____

Library _____

Phone _____

Address _____

Movie theater _____

Phone _____

Address _____

Carpet cleaner _____

Phone _____

Address _____

Window washer _____

Phone _____

Address _____

Hair salon/barber shop _____

Phone _____

Address _____

Other

Name _____

Phone _____

Address _____

_____

Name _____

Phone _____

Address _____

_____

Name _____

Phone _____

Address _____

_____

Name _____

Phone _____

Address _____

New Neighbors Telephone List

Parent's name _____

Child's name _____ Age _____

Child's name _____ Age _____

Phone _____   Cell phone _____

Address _____

Parent's name _____

Child's name _____ Age _____

Child's name _____ Age _____

Phone _____   Cell phone _____

Address _____

Parent's name _____

Child's name _____ Age _____

Child's name _____ Age _____

Child's name _____ Age _____

Phone _____   Cell phone _____

Address _____

Parent's name _____

Child's name _____ Age _____

Child's name _____ Age _____

Child's name _____ Age _____

Phone _____   Cell phone _____

Address _____

Connecting Utilities Worksheet

The following information will be required: name, new address, Social Security number, and new telephone number. Other information may also be requested. **Request your new telephone number first.**

Cable (You may need to request a cable box and remote control.)

Name of provider _____

Phone _____

Service connection date _____

Electric/gas

Name of provider _____

Phone _____

Service connection date _____

Garbage/recycling (Request trash and recycling bins, if available.)

Name of provider _____

Phone _____

Service connection date _____

Heating

Name of provider _____

Phone _____

Service connection date _____

Sewer (Not required if you have a septic tank.)

Name of provider _____

Phone _____

Service connection date _____

Telephone (Refer to telephone service worksheets.)

Name of provider _____

Phone _____

Service connection date _____

Water (Not required if you have a well.)

Name of provider _____

Phone _____

Service connection date _____

Disconnecting Utilities Worksheet

Provide your new address and phone number so that the final bill can be forwarded to you.

Cable (Return cable box and remote control.)

Name of provider _____

Phone _____

Service disconnect date _____

Electric/gas

Name of provider _____

Phone _____

Service stop date _____

Garbage/recycling (Return trash and recycling bins to get deposit refunded.)

Name of provider _____

Phone _____

Service stop date _____

Heating

Name of provider _____

Phone _____

Service stop date _____

Sewer (Not required if you have a septic tank.)

Name of provider _____

Phone _____

Service stop date _____

Telephone

Local provider _____   Phone _____

Long distance provider _____   Phone _____

Service stop date _____

Water (Not required if you have a well.)

Name of provider _____

Phone _____

Service stop date _____

Local Telephone Service Worksheet

Name of local service carrier _____

Phone number _____

Installation department phone number _____

Name of long-distance carrier _____

Phone number _____

Connection date _____

Confirmation number _____

New home phone number _____

Second line phone number _____

Third line phone number _____

Fourth line phone number _____

Voice mail number _____

Temporary pass code (usually 4 digits) _____

Total monthly service fees $ _____
(Flat rate or message rate/low use message rate service plus optional services)

Total connection fees $ _____

Deposit fee $ _____

Do you want your name listed in the phone book?   Yes/No

Name listed as: _____

Optional services (A package rate may be offered for these types of services.)

Home voice mail _____ $ _____

Connection fee _____ $ _____

Local package premium rate _____ $ _____

Touch Tone _____ $ _____

Regional calls _____ $ _____

Calling card _____ $ _____
(calling card identification number, usually 4 digits)

Caller ID, Caller ID with name, and Anonymous

Call Rejection (ACR) _____ $ _____

3-way conference _____ $ _____

*69 _____ $ _____

Ultra Forward service _____ $ _____

Sensible Minute _____ $ _____

Call waiting with tone block _____ $ _____

Call block _____ $ _____

Call forwarding _____ $ _____

Repeat dialing _____ $ _____

Speed dialing _____ $ _____

Home intercom _____ $ _____

Distinctive ring _____ $ _____

Intercom extra _____ $ _____

Guardian (maintenance) plan _____ $ _____

Extra line connection fee _____ $ _____

Package rate   Yes/No

Long-Distance Telephone Service Worksheet

Name of long-distance carrier _____

Carrier phone number _____

Primary phone number _____

Type of calling plan _____

Price per month $ _____

Optional Services

Calling cards   Yes/No

Prepaid calling cards   Yes/No

800 number   Yes/No

_____   Yes/No

_____   Yes/No

Your 800 number   (800) _____

Your access code number _____

Other features requested

_____

_____

_____

_____

_____

_____

_____

_____

_____

_____

Wireless Phone Service Worksheet

Have your cellular phone with you so that it can be reprogrammed to the new number while you are on the phone with your wireless service provider.

Name of wireless service carrier _____

Carrier phone number _____

New service   Yes/No

Transfer of service   Yes/No

Current service account number _____

Current service cell phone number _____

New cell phone number   _____

Local rate per minute: $ _____ per minute

Long distance and roaming rate per minute: $ _____ per minute

Maximum number of minutes per month: _____ minutes for $ _____ per month

Calling plans and features

Name of plan _____

Total rate per month $_____

_____/minutes/month for local calls

_____/minutes for roaming calls

_____/minutes for long distance calls

3-way conference   Yes/No   Rate per month $_____

Caller ID   Yes/No   Rate per month $_____

Voice mail   Yes/No   Rate per month $_____

Special contract terms

_____

_____

_____

Requesting Service Providers Worksheet

Extermination service _____

Phone _____

Service start date _____

Date and time of service _____

Housekeeping service _____

Phone _____

Service start date _____

Date and time of service _____

Lawn service _____

Phone _____

Service start date _____

Date and time of service _____

Newspaper service _____

Phone _____

Service start date _____

Delivery day   Everyday/Only weekdays/Only weekends/Only Sunday

Security system monitoring service _____

Phone _____

Service start date _____

Wireless phone service (Refer to Wireless Phone Service Worksheet.)

Provider _____

Phone _____

Service start date _____

Canceling Service Providers Worksheet

Extermination service _____

Phone _____

Service stop date _____

Housekeeping service _____

Phone _____

Service stop date _____

Lawn service _____

Phone _____

Service stop date _____

Newspaper service _____

Phone _____

Service stop date _____

Security system monitoring service (You may need to request cancellation of this service in writing.)

Provider _____

Phone _____

Service stop date _____

Wireless phone service _____

Phone _____

Account number _____

Service stop date _____

Homeowner's Insurance Quote Worksheet

Typical questions:

1. Age of structure   _____
2. Number of stories   _____
3. Number of fireplaces   _____
4. Number of bathrooms   _____
5. Number of rooms   _____
6. Total square footage of house   _____
7. Property lot size   _____
8. Size of garage   _____
9. Exterior building material   _____
10. Roof material   _____
11. Pool and/or Jacuzzi   _____
12. Gated and locked pool area   Yes/No _____
13. Monitored security system   Yes/No _____
14. Gated community   Yes/No _____
15. Located in a flood plain   Yes/No _____
16. Smoke detectors   Yes/No _____
17. Sales price   _____
18. Mortgage amount   _____
19. Additional floater coverage/$ value   _____
    (For expensive items such as art, antiques, electronics, jewelry, and precious
    stones. A copy of the appraisal certificate will be required.)
20. Closing date   _____
21. Amount of deductible   _____
22. Lender's name/agent   _____
23. Lender's telephone number   _____

Insurance broker/company _____

Name of agent _____

Phone _____

Fax _____

Address _____

Insurance broker/company _____

Name of agent _____

Phone _____

Fax _____

Address _____

Name of insurance company for first quote _____

Name of insurance company for second quote _____

Coverage levels	First quote	Second quote
Dwelling replacement cost	$ _____	$ _____
Other structures	$ _____	$ _____
Personal property	$ _____	$ _____
Loss of use	$ _____	$ _____
Personal liability	$ _____	$ _____
Medical benefit	$ _____	$ _____
Required effective date	$ _____	$ _____

Deductible amount	First quote	Second quote
$500/year	$ _____	$ _____
$1,000/year	$ _____	$ _____
Floater coverage/year	$ _____	$ _____

(Includes appraised valuable items such as art, antiques, electronics, jewelry, and precious stones.)

Automobile Insurance Quote Worksheet

Name of insurance company for first quote _____

Name of agent _____ Phone _____

Name of insurance company for second quote _____

Name of agent _____ Phone _____

Typical questions

1. Year and make of automobile(s)   First automobile _____

   Second automobile _____

2. Number of miles to work?   First automobile _____

   Second automobile _____

3. Any accidents or claims in the past three years? Yes/No   How many? _____

4. Proof of insurance for past year? Yes/No   If not, why? _____

_____

Coverage levels	First quote	Second quote
Bodily injury liability		
Amount per person	$ _____	$ _____
Amount per occurrence	$ _____	$ _____
Property damage liability	$ _____	$ _____
Personal injury protection	$ _____	$ _____
Driver and/or passenger	Covered/Not covered	Covered/Not covered
No fault	Covered/Not covered	Covered/Not covered
Underinsured	Covered/Not covered	Covered/Not covered
Not insured	Covered/Not covered	Covered/Not covered
Extended medical benefits (per person)	$ _____	$ _____

Coverage levels *(continued)*	First quote	Second quote
Deductible for comprehensive coverage	$ _____	$ _____
Deductible for collision coverage	$ _____	$ _____
Towing and labor	Covered/Not covered	Covered/Not covered
Amount per occurrence	$ _____	$ _____
Car rental reimbursement	Covered/Not covered	Covered/Not covered
Amount per day: up to ___ days	$ ____ up to ____ days	$ ____ up to ____ days
Total cost for six months	$ _____	$ _____

Moving Expense Record Worksheet

Item	Total cost	Deposit paid	Balance due
_____	_____	_____	_____
_____	_____	_____	_____
_____	_____	_____	_____
_____	_____	_____	_____
_____	_____	_____	_____
_____	_____	_____	_____
_____	_____	_____	_____
_____	_____	_____	_____
_____	_____	_____	_____
_____	_____	_____	_____
_____	_____	_____	_____
_____	_____	_____	_____
_____	_____	_____	_____
_____	_____	_____	_____
_____	_____	_____	_____
_____	_____	_____	_____
_____	_____	_____	_____
_____	_____	_____	_____
_____	_____	_____	_____
_____	_____	_____	_____
_____	_____	_____	_____
_____	_____	_____	_____
_____	_____	_____	_____
_____	_____	_____	_____
_____	_____	_____	_____

List of Items Damaged in Transit

(Must submit claim form by: _____)

_____

_____

_____

_____

_____

_____

_____

_____

_____

_____

_____

_____

_____

_____

_____

_____

_____

_____

_____

_____

_____

_____

New House Closing Notes

_____

_____

_____

_____

_____

_____

_____

_____

_____

_____

_____

_____

_____

_____

_____

_____

_____

_____

_____

_____

_____

_____

_____

_____

_____

_____

General Notes

List of Items to Replace after the Move

Top-Ten New Places to Explore

1. _____

_____

2. _____

_____

3. _____

_____

4. _____

_____

5. _____

_____

6. _____

_____

7. _____

_____

8. _____

_____

9. _____

_____

10. _____

_____

New House List of Things to Do

1. _____

2. _____

3. _____

4. _____

5. _____

6. _____

7. _____

8. _____

9. _____

10. _____

11. _____

12. _____

13. _____

14. _____

15. _____

16. _____

17. _____

18. _____

19. _____

20. _____

21. _____

22. _____

23. _____

24. _____

25. _____

About the Author

Martha Poage graduated from the University of Delaware and received her MBA from Pepperdine University while working full-time as a senior contract administrator in the aerospace industry in Southern California. She, her husband, and their two children have relocated as her husband's career demanded. She has lived on the East Coast, the West Coast, and several places in between. She currently resides in Scottsdale, Arizona, but is always prepared for the next move.

Martha wrote this moving guide to help her family survive every move and also to help others. She has been known to say, "I cry when I move to a new place, and I cry when I leave."